Collins

SUNDERLAND COLLEGE
0025765

D0988299

tudent Support
Materials for
OCR AS Sociology

CITY OF
LEARNING
CENTRE
SUNDERLAND COLLEGE

Unit G672

ociology of the
amily

Authors: Martin Holborn and Fionnuala Swann
Series editor: Peter Langley

Published by Collins Education
An imprint of HarperCollins Publishers
77-85 Fulham Palace Road
Hammersmith
London
W6 8JB

Browse the complete Collins Education catalogue at
www.collinseducation.com

© HarperCollins Publishers Limited 2011

10 9 8 7 6 5 4 3 2 1

ISBN 978-0-00-741836-7

Martin Holborn and Fionnuala Swann assert their moral rights to be identified as the authors of this work.

All rights reserved. No part of this publication may be reproduced, stored in a retrieval system, or transmitted in any form or by any means, electronic, mechanical, photocopying, recording or otherwise, without the prior written permission of the Publisher or a licence permitting restricted copying in the United Kingdom issued by the Copyright Licensing Agency Ltd, 90 Tottenham Court Road, London W1T 4LP.

British Library Cataloguing in Publication Data.

A Catalogue record for this publication is available from the British Library.

Project editor: Sarah Vittachi

Design and typesetting by Hedgehog Publishing Limited

Cover Design by Angela English

Production by Simon Moore

Printed and bound by L.E.G.O. S.p.A Italy

Indexed by Indexing Specialists (UK) Ltd

Acknowledgements

Every effort has been made to contact the holders of copyright material, but if any have been inadvertently overlooked the publishers will be pleased to make the necessary arrangements at the first opportunity.

p10, fig 2, source: ONS Social Trends 2009; p11, fig 3, source: ONS Social Trends 2009; p12, fig 4, source: Office for National Statistics; p14, source: Office for National Statistics; p15, table 1, source: Office for National Statistics (figures as original source); p16, fig 5, source: Office for National Statistics; p18, fig 6, source: Office for National Statistics, table 2, source: General Household Survey, Office for National Statistics; p34, table 6, source: Office for National Statistics; p35, table 7, source: Office for National Statistics; p39, table 8, source: Office for National Statistics; p40, source: Office for National Statistics; p41, table 9, source: Office for National Statistics; p43, fig 9, source: Jules Shropshire and Sue Middleton, Small Expectations: Learning to be poor? (1999), Joseph Rowntree Foundation; p56, table 12, source: Economic Social Data Service, Universities of Essex and Manchester; p57, table 13, source: Economic Social Data Service, Universities of Essex and Manchester; p58, table 14, source: Jan Pahl, Money and Marriage (1989), Palgrave Macmillan; p60, fig 10, source: Office for National Statistics; p64, fig 11, source: Office for National Statistics, fig 12, source: Office for National Statistics.

Thanks to the following students for providing answers to the questions:

Ruby Barwood, Collette Blackman, Lauren Foley, Vicki Gill, Jessica Gowers, Fran Guratsky, Rachel Hewitt, Ella Keating, Charlotte Ross, Eric Wedge-Bull.

Contents

SUNDERLAND COLLEGE	£5.99
ORDER NO:	LB/1179
DATE	9/13
ACCESSION NO	0025765
RECOMMENDED	P. STA

The family – key concepts

At first sight it seems easy to define the family. Most people could easily identify whom they consider to be members of their family. Usually this will include their mother and father, brothers and sisters, any children and possibly less close relatives such as grandparents, aunts and uncles. We are connected to these individuals either through blood (genetic) links or marriage. People who are connected in these ways can be defined as **kin**. Seeing the family in this way is a common-sense definition of the family, and this was the starting point for the **functionalist** sociologist George Peter Murdock (1949).

Murdock defined the family as 'a social group characterized by common residence, economic cooperation and reproduction. It includes adults of both sexes, at least two of whom maintain a socially approved sexual relationship, and one or more children, own or adopted, of the sexually cohabiting adults'.

Murdock studied 250 societies and claimed the family, as defined above, was present in all of them. He therefore saw it as a **universal** institution (it was found in all societies) that was necessary for the smooth functioning and survival of any society.

Murdock's definition only includes members of the **nuclear family**, which consists of two generations: parents and their immature offspring. He assumed that they are co-resident – or live in the same household.

Murdock's definition can be seen as too narrow for a number of reasons.

1. Not all societies have nuclear families

Research by Kathleen Gough (1959) into the Nayar of southern India found that wives did not live with the man they married (their *tali* **husband**) and instead had several visiting husbands (*sandbanham* **husbands**). Sandbanham husbands slept with a wife but did not live with her permanently. These husbands (who were usually warriors) would arrive at their wife's house at night but would have to leave if another man had arrived first and had left his spear outside the house. Each man could have several wives. In terms of Murdock's definition this society did not possess a family, since fathers did not live with their children.

2. Murdock ignores the importance of the extended family

The **extended family** also includes relations by blood or marriage from other generations (for example, grandparents) and the siblings of parents (aunts and uncles of the children) as well as more distant relatives such as cousins. Extended families may share a common residence (for example, when adult children look after their own parents as well as their children), or they may live apart but keep in touch. When close contacts are kept with kin even though they live apart, this is called an **extended kinship network**.

Examiners' notes

Definitions are invaluable in exams and there are always AO1 marks available for defining your terms, especially in 33-mark questions. It is well worth learning Murdock's definition of the family off by heart and repeating it where appropriate.

Essential notes

The term 'the family' is sometimes used to describe **cohabiting** groups, usually a nuclear family living under the one roof, but can also be used to describe groups related by blood or marriage who do not live together; for example, extended families when the whole family does not share a single residence. Make sure that you specify whether you are describing a co-resident group or not when writing about family types.

3. Some families do not include two adults

In Britain, and elsewhere, it is increasingly common for families to be headed by a lone parent (**lone-parent families**).

Some sociologists believe that lone-parent families form a distinctive family type. In parts of the Caribbean and parts of Central America and the USA a significant proportion of households do not contain an adult male. These **female-headed families**, or **matrifocal families**, are also comparatively common amongst African-Caribbean families in the UK.

The sociologist Nancie Gonzalez (1970) believes that matrifocal families are a well-organized social group which is well adapted to living on a low income. The mothers who head these families often get strong support from female relatives that helps them to cope with raising children.

Yanina Sheeran (1993) believes that the **female carer-core**, consisting of a mother and her children, is the basic family unit. She argues that this family unit is universal. However, a problem with this definition is the existence of male-headed households, where a single father raises children.

4. Some families do not have adults of both sexes

Gay families do not conform to Murdock's definition because they do not contain adults of both sexes, and in some societies the sexual relationship involved might not be approved throughout society. They might, however, include children from a previous heterosexual relationship, or children who have been adopted or produced through **new reproductive technologies**. Sydney Callahan (1997) believes that gay or lesbian households with children should be regarded as families.

In 2005 in the UK, **civil partnerships** (which involve similar legal rights and obligations to marriage) for gay and lesbian couples were legalized, implying that gay and lesbian relationships are now socially accepted and their households should be regarded as families.

Conclusion

Murdock's view on the universal nuclear family is not reflected in Britain today. Sociologists such as Graham Allan and Graham Crow (2001) therefore argue that it has become much more difficult to define 'the family' in Britain today, and there are now a wide variety of family types.

Examiners' notes

The issue of matrifocal families is also important when discussing family diversity and particularly ethnic diversity.

Examiners' notes

The growth of gay and lesbian families is another important aspect of diversity and therefore relevant to questions on that issue.

The ideology of the nuclear family

An **ideology** is a set of distorted beliefs which often serves the interests of one group at the expense of others. Some sociologists believe that the idea that the nuclear family is the normal or best type of family is a type of ideology. This is because it can be used to justify policies or attitudes which disadvantage those who live outside nuclear families and favour those who live inside them.

For example, Diana Gittins (1993) argues that there is no single family type which is found in all societies. The form which families and households take varies widely, so it is not possible to produce a definition of the family which fits all societies. In all societies people have intimate relationships and parents care for their children, but what is classed as a **legitimate** family varies and is influenced by ideological differences.

Two opposing ideological viewpoints on nuclear families in Britain can be identified:

1. **New Right** thinkers tend to support narrow definitions which see nuclear families based around married couples as the only true family type (see page 50). Many supporters of this viewpoint, such as Patricia Morgan (1993), see the family as an institution as under threat. They believe that the stability of society depends upon strong families, with a male **breadwinner** and a female responsible for most of the **domestic labour**.
2. An alternative viewpoint sees all types of family as legitimate. Jeffrey Weeks, Catherine Donovan and Brian Heaphey (1999) are highly critical of what they call the **heteronorm** – the belief that intimate relationships between heterosexual couples are the only legitimate basis on which families can be formed. Instead, they believe that individuals increasingly form **chosen families** – where they can decide whom they choose to regard as being part of the family. Membership might be based upon gay and lesbian relationships or simply friendship.

The cereal packet image of the family

The idea that a single family type is dominant is also found in the media. According to Ann Oakley (1982), marketing and advertising often tries to sell products to what it sees as a typical family. Oakley believes that the image of the typical family presented, for example, in advertising for breakfast cereals, portrays the conventional family as 'nuclear families composed of legally married couples, voluntarily choosing the parenthood of one or more (but not too many) children'. Edmund Leach (1967) calls this the **cereal packet image of the family**.

The cereal packet image of the family has been attacked by the American feminist Barrie Thorne (1992). Thorne believes that gender, generation, **ethnicity** and **class** result in widely varying experiences of family life, many of which diverge from the nuclear family with the male breadwinner and female **housewife**.

Examiners' notes

In both 17- and 33-mark questions, the addition of theoretical content will help you get towards or into the top mark bands, as it is regarded as a good source of sociological evidence. You could add more details on the New Right using the material on pages 50–51.

Examiners' notes

In essay questions it is worth mentioning the cereal packet image of the family when discussing a range of issues, including debates about the popularity and influence of the nuclear family, discussions on family diversity and questions on conjugal roles.

Problems with the ideology

The **feminist** writers Michele Barrett and Mary McIntosh (1982) criticize the ideology of the nuclear family for making the assumption that the only satisfying way to live is in this type of family. This devalues relationships outside the family; for example, in residential homes and houses shared by students. There is no intrinsic reason why living arrangements outside of conventional families should not be satisfying and fulfilling.

Most sociologists believe that no one single family type is dominant in the UK and they do not see this as a bad thing. Supporters of increasing **diversity** such as Robert and Rhona Rapoport (1982) see greater diversity as a good thing because it gives people more freedom to choose how to live their lives. From this viewpoint, any **household** with intimate relationships can be seen as a family regardless of the exact combination of adults and children who live within it.

The influence of family ideology

Although the idea of the nuclear family as the dominant type of family may be seen as an ideology, it has still has considerable influence. For example, it has influenced a range of family policies put forward by different political parties. Graham Allan (1985) claims that everything from education policy (which assumes one parent will be at home to meet the children after school) to housing policy (which supports the provision of family-sized houses) is based on the assumption that the single-earner nuclear family is the norm.

Politicians often stress the importance of the family. Before becoming prime minister at the head of the Coalition Government in 2010, David Cameron emphasized that he wanted tax breaks to help married couples and their families.

Examiners' notes

Both feminist theories and the development of diversity are discussed in much more detail in other sections (see pp 28–31 and pp 34–37). Both of these points could be developed to include greater evaluation in an essay.

Essential notes

A variety of politicians from all the main parties have made speeches arguing for the importance of nuclear families, but Conservative politicians tend to be more strongly in favour of traditional families than those from other parties. However, once in power, a party's policies are often more ambiguous than just supporting nuclear families.

Extended families

Definition of the extended family

Extended families include **kin** in addition to the members of the **nuclear family**; for example, a third generation of grandparents as well as parents and children. They may also include the siblings of adults or cousins, so the family extends beyond immediate kin in the same generation.

The ideology of the nuclear family suggests that in Britain today extended families are no longer very important. A range of research has examined whether the nuclear or extended family has been dominant in Britain over recent decades and some has questioned this view. This tradition of research was pioneered by Michael Young and Peter Willmott (1957), who first studied family life in London during the 1950s.

> ### Key study
>
> ### Young and Willmott – the extended and nuclear family
>
> Studying family life in Bethnal Green (East London) in the 1950s, Willmott and Young found there was a strong bond between married daughters and their mothers, who often lived close together, even if not under the same roof. This family type demonstrated close-knit **extended kinship networks.**
>
> In the 1970s they found that the nuclear family had become dominant. It was based on a strong **conjugal bond** between husband and wife, and other relatives outside the nuclear family lost importance. Willmott and Young described this as a **symmetrical family**. By this they meant that the husband and wife have similar roles; both do paid work and both do housework and childcare. It developed because:
>
> * rising wages and a developing **welfare state** made nuclear families more self-reliant
> * increased **geographical mobility** affected kinship networks
> * entertainment and facilities in the home improved
> * families became smaller, with fewer children per couple.

Extended families in the 1980s and 1990s

Willmott and Young's research suggested that the extended family would become less and less important as time went on, but some research contradicts this.

Francis McGlone et al. (1996) argue that kin outside the nuclear family are important because they can provide both practical and emotional support. For example, the parents of married children might offer:

* advice
* financial help
* assistance with childcare
* emotional support in times of crisis.

Although kin may live some distance apart, rising living standards, growing car ownership and technological developments make it much easier to

> **Examiners' notes**
>
> Look out for 17-mark questions on the reasons for changes such as this. Your explanation of reasons for the changes will need to be developed. For example, you could expand on the reasons for smaller family size using material from pages 12–14.

> **Examiners' notes**
>
> Class differences are important as an aspect of diversity, so make sure you mention differences in extended family networks if you are asked about this.

keep in touch and to visit one another. McGlone found that contacts remained frequent, with the **working class** having more contact with kin than the **middle class**.

Research findings on the importance of family life

Research suggests that most people continue to attach a great deal of importance to family life, are family-centred and usually maintain contact with kin who live elsewhere.

- McGlone found that most parents believed they should continue to support their children even after they had left home.
- Data from the British Social Attitudes Survey (2001) showed that only about 10% of adults did not see their parents frequently and over 60% of grandparents saw their grandchildren at least once a week.
- The British Social Attitudes Survey (2005) shows that the majority of both men (57%) and women (65%) see family members or other relatives weekly or nearly every week. Relatives and friends are about equally important in terms of social contacts, with work colleagues and other acquaintances being much less important. Only a small percentage of men (5%) and women (2%) very rarely or never see other family members.

Examiners' notes

This research contrasts rather with research suggesting diversity is becoming the norm – it could be used to add evaluation to 33-mark questions on growing diversity.

Family structures in contemporary society

A variety of descriptions have been used to characterize family structures in contemporary Britain:

- Peter Willmott (1988) sees the **dispersed extended family** as typical. Most people live in nuclear families, but contacts with extended family members who may live some distance apart remain important.
- Julia Brannen (2003) uses the term **beanpole family** to describe families today. She believes there are strong **intergenerational** links between grandparents, children and grandchildren, but links with siblings and cousins (**intragenerational** links) are much less important.
- Margaret O'Brien and Deborah Jones (1996) found in research in East London that no one family type is now dominant. Instead there is a **pluralization of lifestyles**. It was therefore pointless to try and find a single family type because family **diversity** is now the norm (see page 34).

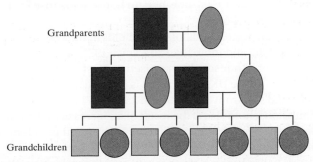

Grandparents

Grandchildren

Examiners' notes

The beanpole family is identified as an important concept in the specification.

Fig 1
Beanpole family structure

Examiners' notes

The difference between households and families is a basic distinction which is invaluable for providing some basic analysis on a wide range of questions.

Trends in household and family size

Family and non-family households

- A **household** consists of one or more people using or sharing accommodation, living and eating together. In Britain, according to government definitions, a household can include unrelated people who are financially or socially independent.
- However, a family is defined as 'a couple (with or without children) or a lone parent with children' (*Social Trends*, 2009).
- As the figure below shows, there are different types of family household, including those that contain an extended or nuclear family. They may also contain more than one family or non-family member.
- Non-family households may contain one or several people. Non-family households are usually communal establishments such as halls of residence or nursing homes.

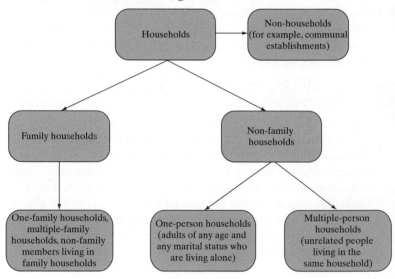

Fig 2
Family and non-family households

Trends in households

Between 1998 and 2008, the percentage of people in family households decreased while the percentage of people in non-family households increased. This is in line with longer-term trends:

- Between 1971 and 1998, **one-person households** rose from 18% to 29% of all households.
- In 2008 there were 35 million households in the UK, an increase of 2% since 2007 and more than 30% since 1971.
- The number of households has risen at a faster rate than the population of the UK. In part, this is due to a fall in average household size from 3.1 in 1961 to 2.9 in 1971 and 2.4 in 2008.
- Falling household size is the result of an increase in the number of one-person households, an increase in the number of **lone-parent households** and a decline in family size. There are a variety of reasons behind each of these trends, which are discussed on page 11.

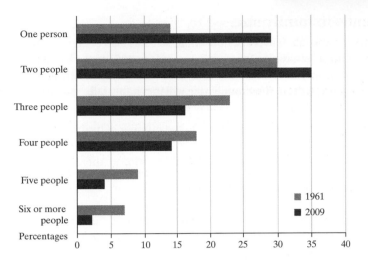

Fig 3
Households and families: the average household size in Great Britain has fallen from 3.1 to 2.4 people over 40 years

Essential notes

An important trend revealed in these figures is the rapid decline in large households. In just under 50 years, the proportion of five-person households approximately halved, and the percentage of 6+ households more than halved to less than 3%.

Reasons for the increase in one-person households

- A significant proportion of one-person households consists of older people who are widows or widowers. Due to increasing **life expectancy** there are growing numbers of elderly people living alone. With the greater life expectancy of women than men, most such households consist of a single female whose partner has died.
- The fastest growth in one-person households has been amongst younger adults. In these age groups, living alone is more common amongst men than women, partly because women are more likely to be lone parents than men and therefore living with one or more children.
- Rising **divorce rates** have led to more people who were formerly married setting up a household on their own.
- There is increased geographical mobility as people, particularly graduates, move to find suitable employment and then live on their own before meeting a partner.
- Rising living standards make it more feasible for people to live on their own since they can afford to pay rent or a mortgage with just one income (although rising house prices have made this difficult in some parts of the country).
- Greater employment opportunities for women have made it more likely that young women can afford to live alone.

The increase may also be driven by changing attitudes as people become more **individualistic** and seek greater freedom and choice in their lives. Sociologists such as Anthony Giddens (1991), Ulrich Beck and Elisabeth Beck-Gernsheim (1995) and Judith Stacey (1996) all believe there are significant trends in society today which lead to people seeking and expecting greater independence (see pages 47–49).

Examiners' notes

This material is also useful for discussing family diversity.

Examiners' notes

This is a typical issue for a 17-mark question. You will only get into the top mark band if you include a range and depth of knowledge and understanding of theories and/or concepts and/or evidence. With that in mind, choose reasons that you can expand on in this way (for example, the final point allows theoretical development).

Essential notes

The birth rate is the number of live births per thousand of the population per year.

The fertility rate is the number of live births per thousand women aged 15 to 44 per year.

The total fertility rate is the number of children each woman has.

Examiners' notes

Make sure that you can define the various rates mentioned above so that you can be precise and pick up marks for knowledge and understanding in both shorter and longer questions.

Essential notes

Migration refers to both people entering a country (**immigration**) and the number of people leaving the country (**emigration**). **Net migration** is the difference between the numbers entering and leaving the country.

Examiners' notes

All of these issues are so closely linked that the same material can often be used to answer questions on any of them.

Trends in family size

Alongside the fall in average household size has also been a fall in family size. Average family size fell from 3.1 people in 1961 to 2.4 in 2008. Family size is primarily affected by the **birth rate** and the **fertility rate**. If women have fewer children, then family size will inevitably fall.

The birth rate

There has been a long-term decline in the number of births in the UK and also in the birth rate. In 2008 there were 790 000 live births in the UK, whereas in 1901, when the population was significantly lower, there were 1 093 000.

Total fertility rate

Fig 4
Live births, England and Wales, 1959–2009

The fertility rate

Much of the decline in the birth rate has been the result of a declining fertility rate. The total fertility rate has declined from 3.5 in 1900 to 1.7 in 1997, though in 2009 it rose slightly to 1.94.

This recent rise in fertility is partly due to patterns of **migration**, with immigrants to the UK tending to have slightly larger families than non-immigrants. It has also been affected by rising fertility rates in older women, some of which may be due to improvements in fertility treatments such as IVF.

Reasons for the long-term decline in family size, birth and fertility rates

1. Changes in gender roles

A major part of the decline can be explained in terms of women choosing to have fewer children. As their role in society has changed, many women are choosing to delay childbearing and to limit the number of children they have. Factors include:

- Improved contraception from the 1960s, which gave women more control over their own fertility.
- Easier access to abortion.

- Women are less likely to get married than in the past and **cohabiting** women are less likely to have children than married women.
- An increase in the number of women in paid employment, particularly after marriage, so that more women delay or limit childbearing to fit in with careers.
- Improved female performance in education and increasing educational opportunities.
- More opportunities for women in employment because of the growth of the service sector.
- Greater legal equality for women, such as the Equal Pay Act (1970), which has made working more worthwhile.
- Difficulty combining work with the care of a large number of children in **dual-earner families**.

Examiners' notes

Look out for this cropping up as a 17-mark question. (It could also feature in essays.) Each of the four reasons here gives you plenty of scope for developing the point and including theory, concepts and evidence.

A decline in the birth and fertility rates may be largely a matter of choice, particularly the choice of women. Although fertility rates amongst older age groups have been rising, women who delay the birth of their first child until they are relatively old may not remain fertile long enough to have large numbers of children.

2. Falling infant mortality

The **infant mortality rate** has fallen dramatically as a result of factors such as rising living standards, improved hygiene and sanitation, improvements in healthcare, and improved monitoring of child welfare as a result of the development of the welfare state.

Essential notes

The infant mortality rate is the number of children dying before their first birthday per thousand live births.

Geographers argue that these circumstances have led to a demographic revolution in which the birth and fertility rates fall because women no longer feel they need to have a large number of children to protect against the risk of infant mortality.

3. Children as an economic burden

In the early 19th century children were often seen as an economic asset because it was possible to send them out to work so that they could contribute to the family income at a relatively early age. However, legislation has gradually banned or restricted the opportunities for children to work, and the length of time children spend in schooling has gradually increased. This has made children economically dependent upon their parents for longer and means they now represent an economic cost rather than an economic asset. As people expect and desire rising living standards, they have less incentive to have several children.

In addition, the development of welfare provision for the elderly has made parents less dependent upon children for care and support in old age.

☞ This topic continues on the next two pages

4. Changing attitudes

Attitudes towards children and childhood have changed. Families and society in general have become more **child-centred**, that is, more concerned with the well-being of children, than they were in the past. As social norms about what constitutes adequate childcare have changed, the time and costs involved in raising children have increased. This has further reduced the economic attractiveness of having large numbers of children. Instead, parents are more likely to concentrate their efforts on raising a small number of children as well as they can.

Ulrich Beck and Elisabeth Beck-Gernsheim (1995) argue that changing attitudes are linked to a process of **individualization.** People no longer have to follow traditional norms and values – instead they make their own decisions. These decisions include whether or not to get married, whether to stay married and whether to have children. Uncertainty and the risk of relationship breakdown make people wary of having too many children. Ironically, however, the children that people do have become increasingly important to them since parent–child relationships are permanent, while marriages may be temporary.

Examiners' notes

Referring to Beck and Beck-Gernsheim gives you the chance to include some advanced theory in answers.

The effects of changes in fertility

Changes in fertility can have a number of consequences for society. These include:

- *Changes in the dependency ratio*. The **dependency ratio** is the ratio between the economically productive part of the population and non-workers or dependents such as children and the elderly. Falling fertility rates reduce the number of dependent children in the short term but in the long term lead to fewer adults of working age. This can increase the proportion of the population who are dependent.
- *Impact on public services such as education*. Falling number of births can lead to the closure of maternity units and schools, which can create problems if the birth rate increases later.
- *Contribution to changes in gender roles*. Women have more time to devote to their careers and this can lead to greater equality in conjugal relationships.

Examiners' notes

You are more likely to get a 17-mark question than a 33-mark question on this area.

Family households – children living with parents

Not all trends have led to a decline in family size. One trend that has counteracted this is an increase in the number of non-dependent children living with their parents. In 2009, 25% of men and 13% of women aged 25 to 29 were living with their parents (ONS, 2009).

Travis (2009) attributes this trend to:

- *Problems in the housing market*. Longer-term rises in property values has priced many young adults out of the property market, with the costs of both renting and purchasing houses becoming prohibitive (especially in the most expensive areas of the country such as London). This is particularly true for young adults on low incomes.

- *The growth of higher education.* Increasing numbers of young people have been continuing in higher education in the UK rather than entering employment. For some graduates, when they have completed their degree and in many cases accumulated considerable debt, a period living with parents may be the only affordable option.
- *Problems in the labour market.* The recent recession and cuts in government spending have led to a shortage of employment opportunities for young people entering the labour market. This has encouraged them to live with parents before establishing a career.
- *Age of marriage.* The relatively late age at which people are getting married, starting to cohabit and having children.

The table below shows the percentage of women with children in the household in 2007 in Great Britain.

Percentages of women with:	Dependent children	Non-dependent children only	No children
Married	53%	16%	31%
Non-married			
Cohabiting	44%	4%	52%
Single	18%	-	81%
Widowed	15%	35%	51%
Divorced	37%	23%	41%
Separated	65%	9%	26%
All working-age women (women aged 16 to 59)	42%	11%	47%

Table 1
Percentage of women with children in the household, Great Britain, 2007

Essential notes

The marriage rate is the number of people per thousand of the single population getting married each year.

Examiners' notes

You can use data on the changes in marriage rates to answer questions that ask you to discuss increasing cohabitation. (Cohabiting couples are, by definition, not married.) Try to remember some simple statistics that will give you solid support for the points you are making.

Trends in marriage and cohabitation

Marriage rates

As early as the 1980s, Robert Chester (1985) noted that marriage rates were falling in many Western countries, including the USA and most of Western Europe.

Fig 5 shows trends in first marriage in England and Wales since 1862. This shows that despite a rising population the number of marriages has decreased considerably since the 1940s. In 2006 there were 237 000 marriages in England and Wales, which was the lowest recorded number since 1895.

Between 1995 and 2005, marriage rates fell from just under 35 males marrying per thousand unmarried males, to under 25 per thousand.

One reason for a decline in marriage rates may be a delay in the timing of marriage, with both men and women tending to postpone their first marriage until later in life. Between 1996 and 2006, age at first marriage rose from 29.3 to 31.8 years amongst men, and from 27.2 to 29.7 years amongst women.

However, it is not just a question of delaying marriage. Each successive generation is less likely to get married, with first marriage rates declining in all age groups. Research by Ben Wilson and Steve Smallwood (2007) shows that rates of marriage in England and Wales have fallen for the **cohorts** of women born in each year between 1974 and 1986.

Fig 5
Trends in first marriage in England and Wales since 1862

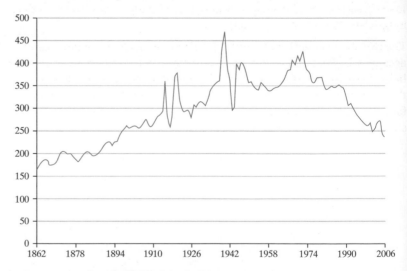

Explanations for declining marriage rates

Declining marriage rates may be caused by several factors which have made marriage less popular. These include:

- Changing social attitudes, which see marriage as less socially desirable than in the past and living outside marriage as more acceptable.

Examiners' notes

A useful tip to get in the top mark band for both 17- and 33-mark questions is to include some theoretical content. If appropriate, make reference to theories of modernity and postmodernity.

- Decline in religious belief (**secularization**), which weakens commitment to marriage as an institution.
- An increase in **cohabitation** (see below).
- A greater emphasis on **individualism** (see p 47).

Declining marriage rates do not necessarily indicate a decline in commitment to long-term relationships; for example:

- Wilson and Smallwood (2007) point out that marriage rates do not include people married abroad and there is an increasing trend for British couples to travel outside the country to marry.
- **Civil partnerships** among gay and lesbian couples have increased.

Cohabitation

Cohabitation has increased rapidly. According to the General Household Survey, in 1979 in the UK less than 3% of females were cohabiting, but by 2005 this had risen to more than 12%.

In 2004/5 amongst cohabiting women, 27% were single (not ever married), 29% divorced, 23% separated and 6% widowed.

Patricia Morgan (2003) sees rising cohabitation as part of a trend in which marriage is going out of fashion. Rather than being a prelude to marriage, Morgan believes that cohabitation represents an increase in the number of sexual partners and the frequency of partner change. She notes that cohabiting couples tend to stay together for a shorter time than married couples.

Joan Chandler (1993) disagrees, seeing cohabitation as a relatively stable, long-term alternative to marriage.

The British Social Attitudes Survey (2001) found evidence of increasing acceptance of cohabitation outside marriage, with younger age groups being more likely to find it acceptable than older age groups. However, these surveys have also found that there continues to be strong support for long-term, heterosexual relationships. On average, cohabitants in the survey had lived together for six and a half years.

Examiners' notes

You can often get extra marks for making methodological points. This point raised by Wilson and Smallwood can be used to question the validity of statistics on marriage rates.

Essential notes

Morgan supports **New Right** theories (see pages 50–51) of the family and she argues that these changes are part of a pattern of moral decline. She would prefer a return to longer relationships, preferably within marriage. Supporters of diversity, however, see these changes as a welcome increase in individual choice.

Trends in divorce, marital breakdown and remarriage

Types of marital breakdown

Marital breakdown involves the failure or ending of a marriage. It can be divided into three main categories:

1. **Divorce** – the legal ending of a marriage.
2. **Separation** – the physical separation of spouses so that they live apart.
3. **'Empty-shell' marriages** – husbands and wives continue to live together and remain legally married but the relationship has broken down.

Trends in divorce

Long-term, the **divorce rate** (the number of people divorcing per thousand of the married population) has risen dramatically. In 1911 there were just 859 petitions for divorce in England and Wales, but in 2008 there were more than 143,000.

More recently there has been some decline in divorce, with the rate in 2008 the lowest since 1979.

Essential notes

If you aren't sure of the definition of a rate, it is worth remembering that rates in this topic are usually defined as per thousand per year of the relevant group.

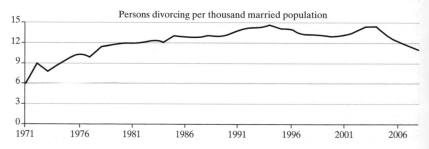

Persons divorcing per thousand married population

Fig 6
Divorces in England and Wales, 1971–2008

Divorce is becoming more likely for women of recent generations than those of older generations. Table 2 shows that in recent cohorts, marriage breakdown for women by the time they had reached 25 had become twice as likely than it was for the cohorts now 25 to 30 years older than them. However, marriage and the birth of a child by that age have become less common. The table provides some evidence of a slight decline in marriage breakdown by the age of 25 for the most recent cohorts, but this will be partly because fewer women had married by that age. (Cohabitation rates have increased dramatically for each cohort.)

Table 2
Experience of family events by women in the UK when aged 25: by age in 2001–03

Age	55–59	50–54	45–49	40–44	35–39	30–34	25–29
Marriage	75%	72%	65%	56%	45%	33%	24%
Birth of child	51%	44%	39%	34%	33%	29%	30%
Cohabitation	1%	2%	4%	7%	12%	16%	21%
Marriage breakdown	6%	7%	11%	14%	14%	13%	13%

Patterns of divorce

The official figures for England and Wales show that in 2008:

- The mean (average) age of divorce for men was 43 and for women 41.
- The **median** duration of marriage was 11.5 years.
- In nearly a third of marriages at least one partner had been previously widowed or divorced.
- 28% of men divorcing and 20% of women divorcing had been married and divorced previously.
- 67% of divorce decrees were awarded to women and 33% to men.
- 50% of couples divorcing had at least one child under 16.

Separation statistics

There are no reliable figures for separation from year to year in Britain. However, the 2001 census found that around 2% of individuals are separated and living alone in Britain. Judicial separations are now uncommon because divorce is easier to obtain and both partners are more likely to accept divorce than in the past.

Empty-shell marriages

There are no reliable estimates of the number of empty-shell marriages. This is partly because it is very difficult to define empty-shell marriages and to operationalize any definition when conducting research.

However, impressionistic historical evidence does suggest that in the past people were more likely to accept an unsatisfactory marriage than today because divorce was almost impossible to obtain in the 19th century.

Explanations for marital breakdown

Nicky Hart (1976) points out that explaining marital breakdown can involve three types of factor:

1. factors affecting the value attached to marriage
2. factors affecting the degree of conflict between spouses
3. factors affecting opportunities to escape from marriage.

The value of marriage

The functionalist Ronald Fletcher (1966) believed that divorce has increased because people attach more value to marriage than in the past. If marriage is so important to individuals, they are more likely to seek divorce if their marriage is unsatisfactory.

The British Social Attitudes Survey (2007) found that people do continue to value marriage but there is no evidence that the value attached to marriage has been *increasing*. Furthermore, cohabitation is increasingly accepted as an alternative to marriage.

Conflict between spouses

A number of possible reasons for increasing conflict between spouses have been put forward.

- Functionalists such as William Goode (1971) believe that conflict has increased because the nuclear family is becoming more isolated from other kin, placing an emotional burden on husbands and wives who have little support from other relatives.

This topic continues on the next two pages

Examiners' notes

The high proportion of divorces initiated by women is sometimes used as evidence by feminists to support the view that women are disadvantaged and exploited within marriage. However, when answering a question on feminism you can also make the point that it has become easier for women to escape unsatisfactory marriages.

Essential notes

Operationalizing means the measurement of abstract concepts by defining them in research; for example, by writing questionnaire questions. Divorce is easy to measure because it is defined legally, but separation and empty-shell marriages are harder to define and measure.

Examiners' notes

The problems of defining the different types of marital breakdown can be used to make the point that the validity of all of the statistics for measuring total marital breakdowns is open to question.

Examiners' notes

To get into the top mark band for both 17- and 33-mark questions, it is useful to make some links between these points and functionalist theory in general.

- Graham Allan and Graham Crowe (2001) believe marital breakdown has increased because the family is less likely to be an **economic unit** (for example, running a family firm), making it easier for spouses to split up.

Modernity, freedom and choice

Colin Gibson (1994) links increased marital breakdown to **modernity**. He argues that individual competition and a free-market economy have placed increased emphasis on **individualism**. Individuals pursue personal satisfaction and are accustomed to the idea of consumer choice and fulfilment coming from such choice. Marriage is therefore treated like other consumer products, and if it is not providing satisfaction it is more likely to be discarded.

The ease of divorce

Changing social attitudes have made it easier for people to contemplate divorce:

- Divorce has become more socially acceptable. The British and European Social Attitudes Survey (1998) found that 82% of people in Britain disagreed that married couples should stay together even if they didn't get along.
- Gibson believes that **secularization** (the decline of religious belief) has loosened the rigid morality which in the past made divorce morally unacceptable to some people.
- Gibson also argues that society lacks shared values which may operate to stabilize marriage.

A wide range of laws have been introduced which make divorce both easier and cheaper to obtain. These laws have undoubtedly affected the divorce rate. For example, the Divorce Reform Act of 1971 removed the idea that one party had to be found guilty of some form of misbehaviour to allow divorce. This was followed by a large increase in divorce as more couples took advantage of the easier process of divorcing. Changing divorce laws are summarized below.

Changing divorce law

- *Pre-1857*: divorce available via Act of Parliament only. Expensive, so few took place.
- *1857 Matrimonial Causes Act*: idea of matrimonial offence created, with adultery as main grounds for divorce, making it easier and cheaper.
- *1950 Divorce Law*: grounds widened to include cruelty and desertion; divorce still based upon blame of one spouse.
- *Divorce Reform Act 1971*: main grounds for divorce now 'irretrievable breakdown' of marriage, making divorce easier and without blame.
- *Divorce Law 1984*: divorce petition period reduced from three years to one, with partners' behaviour taken into account in financial settlement. Divorce became quicker.
- *Family Law Act 1996*: no longer any need to prove irretrievable breakdown; partners could simply state that the marriage had

Essential notes

You can develop Gibson's point further by linking it to the ideas of Ulrich Beck and Anthony Giddens, whose theories suggest a similar relationship between modernity and changes in personal relationships (see page 47).

broken down, with divorce finalized after a period of reflection. Aimed to increase stability of marriage, but in some ways made divorce easier.

Divorce has become a more affordable proposition as a result of changes in laws which affect the cost of getting a divorce or provide for those who have been divorced:

- In 1949 the Legal Aid and Advice Act provided for free advice for those who could not afford to pay a solicitor.
- The Child Support, Pensions and Social Security Act of 2000 laid down fixed contributions that absent parents had to pay for their children, making it easier for parents (usually the mother) to retain some economic security after divorce.

Remarriage

Although divorce rates seem to indicate a decline in the popularity of marriage, high rates of remarriage after divorce suggest that it is particular marriages that many people are rejecting rather than the idea of marriage itself.

Remarriages have been increasing as a proportion of all marriages. In 1996, 39% of marriages were a remarriage for one or both partners; by 2006 this had risen to 42%. Before the 1971 Divorce Reform Act remarriages were comparatively rare but, not surprisingly, they have risen as an increasing number of people have got divorced and therefore become available for remarriage.

Examiners' notes

It is important to learn some of the key dates and changes in legislation to give substance to answers on reasons for these key trends or for increasing diversity. Referring to legal changes helps to show that you understand that the changing rates of divorce might reflect changing laws as much as changing attitudes to marriage.

Examiners' notes

Don't assume that all lone parents are women. A minority of lone-parent households are headed by men. Make it clear that you are aware of this in the way you phrase responses.

Trends in parenting

There are two key trends in parenting:

1. An increase in the number of lone parents.
2. A tendency towards becoming a parent later in life.

The growth of lone parenthood

Lone parenthood can come about through a number of different routes. People who are married can become lone parents through **divorce**, **separation** or the death of a spouse. Similarly, **cohabiting** parents who are not married and have children can split up or one of them die. It can also result from births to women who do not live with the father of the child.

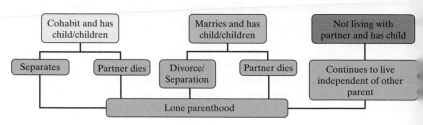

Fig 7
Paths into lone parenthood

In 2007, nearly one in five single women, and more than a third of divorced women who were not cohabiting with a man, lived with a dependent child or children.

Lone-parent households have grown rapidly over recent decades, with government statistics for the United Kingdom showing that between 1971 and 2008 the percentage of households consisting of lone parents and dependent children has risen from 3% to 7%.

Reasons for the increase in lone parenthood

There are basically two reasons for the increase in lone parenthood:

1. The increase in divorce, which leaves more parents (usually mothers) bringing up children on their own.
2. The increase in the number of single, never-married parents (overwhelmingly mothers).

The reasons for this are explored in more detail on pp 42–43.

Delaying parenthood

Although a significant number of mothers become lone parents at a young age, in general the trend in Britain is towards having children later in life.

Government figures for England and Wales show that:

- The age of women at the birth of their first child has risen from 23.7 in 1971, to 26.1 in 1997 and 29.3 in 2007.
- The average age of women giving birth rose from 26.6 in 1971, to 28.3 in 1997 and almost 30 (29.3) in 2007.

Reasons for later parenthood

Research by Gloria Gonzalez-Lopez (2002) has found that, throughout Europe, women are tending to give birth to their first child later in life, and the average age at which they give birth in general has been increasing.

Examiners' notes

Is very useful to remember simple statistics such as the overall percentage increase so that you can include some hard, statistical evidence in your answers.

Essential notes

Both of these factors may be linked to female liberation as a result of the growth of feminism and the growth of individualism explored in the theories of Anthony Giddens and Ulrich Beck and Elisabeth Beck-Gernsheim.

According to Gonzalez-Lopez, later age at birth is linked to two factors:

- *Greater female participation in the labour market,* with women wishing to develop careers before having their first child or delaying having a subsequent child in order to avoid career breaks which are too long to provide opportunities for promotion.
- *Higher levels of educational achievement.* There is a strong relationship between level of education and delaying childbirth. The increasing proportion of women staying on in education and gaining degrees might therefore help to explain later childbirth amongst women in Britain.

Another factor which might be important is the development of reliable methods of contraception since the 1960s, which make it easier for women to control the timing of childbirth.

Whatever the explanations for later childbirth and the related trend of small family size, it has implications for relationships within the family. These are discussed in later sections.

Functionalist theories of the family

The functionalist perspective

Functionalists see society as an interrelated whole. To functionalists every institution in society performs one or more important **functions** or jobs and they assume that this helps society to run smoothly like a well-oiled machine. Functionalist theories of the family therefore look for the positive benefits and functions that the family performs for all societies.

George Peter Murdock – the universal functions of the family

As discussed on p4, Murdock (1949) believed that the nuclear family is a **universal** institution vital to the well-being of all societies. From his study of 250 societies, he identified four functions of the family:

1. The **sexual function**. The family prevents disruption to society by limiting sexuality to monogamous relationships, preventing the conflict that might otherwise result from sexual desire.
2. The **reproductive function**. The family ensures the reproduction of a new generation vital for the survival of society.
3. The **economic function**. The family acts as an economic unit, ensuring the survival of its members by providing food and shelter.
4. The **educational function.** The family provides a stable environment in which children can be socialized into the culture of their society.

Parsons – the basic and irreducible functions of the family

Talcott Parsons (1959, 1965) studied American society and found that even though the family had lost some functions (see below), it retains two 'basic and irreducible functions':

1. **Primary socialization**. The family was the only institution in which **primary socialization** (the first and most important stage of socialization) could take place effectively so that children would internalize the norms and values of their society.
2. **Stabilization of adult personalities**. In Western societies the **isolated nuclear family** gets little support from **extended kinship networks**. The stress of the competitive world of work for the husband can be counterbalanced by the warmth and security offered by the nuclear family, and within the family adults can act out the childish elements in their personalities. This helps to stabilize their personalities.

Parsons – changing family structure

Parsons believed that the structure of the family changes to fit the needs of different types of society.

In **pre-industrial societies** the **extended family** was the norm. Most people worked in agriculture and the extended family worked the land together. In industrial society the **nuclear family** of parents and children developed. The nuclear family was necessary because:

1. Industry required a **geographically mobile** workforce which could move to where new factories were being built, and this was difficult to achieve with large extended families.

Examiners' notes

It is important to memorize the functions of the family identified by Murdock and Parsons. They form the starting point for any answer about functionalism.

2. A **socially mobile** workforce was also necessary. In extended families **status** was largely **ascribed** (given by birth), with the eldest males having high status. This could cause problems if a younger male had a higher **achieved status** because he had a better job. Nuclear families without extended kin avoided this problem.

Talcott Parsons – changing functions of the family.

Parsons argues that as society changes, the family loses some of its functions. In pre-industrial times it carried out many functions, but in **industrial society** specialist institutions take over some of these functions. This process is called **structural differentiation**.

For example, health care and support for the family used to be the responsibility of the family. Now the welfare state has taken over much of the responsibility.

Criticisms of functionalism

The functionalist view of the family has been heavily criticized for being outdated and for presenting an overly optimistic view of family life. Criticisms include the following:

Functionalist view	Criticism
Family has unique functional role	Some societies do not have traditional families
Family is functional for all members	Ignores 'dark side', e.g. domestic violence, sexual abuse
Family unit benefits all members	Feminists argue that men benefit more than women
Families and society benefit from men being main breadwinners and women main carers	Feminists view this as patriarchal and sexist
Dominant family type has shifted from extended to nuclear	Ignores evidence of non-dominance of the extended family in the pre-industrial era, and decline of nuclear family and increasing family diversity
Nuclear family best adapted to modern society	Postmodernists argue there are many viable alternatives

Table 3
Criticisms of the functionalist view

Examiners' notes
Parsons' views on changes in the family with industrialization are essential for understanding later debates on how the family has changed. For 33-mark questions in particular the evaluation of extended family networks on page 8, which shows that they have remained important, will be useful.

Essential notes
The functionalist Ronald Fletcher (1966) believed that the family developed some new functions such as acting as a unit of consumption – goods are bought for families as a whole. Fletcher also believed that the family retains important functions in education and health, supplementing and supporting the job done by schools, doctors and hospitals.

Examiners' notes
All the main perspectives (Marxism, feminism, the New Right and postmodernism) can be used to criticize functionalism. When revising it is important to identify similarities and differences between all the main perspectives. The table of criticisms is not exhaustive; as you work through the material think about other ways that functionalism can be criticized.

Marxist theories of the family

Introduction to Marxism

According to Karl Marx (1818–1883) and Frederick Engels (1820–1895) power in society largely stemmed from wealth. In particular, those who owned the **means of production** (the things needed to produce other things such as land, capital, machinery and labour power) formed a powerful **ruling class**. They were able to exploit the **subject class** (those who did not own the means of production and therefore had to work for the ruling class).

Economic systems

According to Marx, society passed through several periods in which different economic systems or **modes of production** were dominant. In each of these there was a different ruling class and subject class. In the latest stage, **capitalist society**, the ruling class were wealthy factory owners (the **bourgeoisie**) and the subject class were the working-class employees (the **proletariat**). In capitalism, the proletariat was exploited by the bourgeoisie because they were not paid for the full value of the work that they did and the bourgeoisie kept some **surplus value** or profit.

The economic base and superstructure

The power of the bourgeoisie derived from their ownership of the means of production. The means of production forms the **economic base** or infrastructure of society. Because they controlled the economic base, the bourgeoisie were able to control the other, non-economic, institutions of society (which make up the **superstructure**) such as the media, government, religion and the family.

> **Examiners' notes**
>
> It is important to use technical terms from Marxist theory (such as means of production) when answering exam questions.

> **Examiners' notes**
>
> The economic base/ superstructure model of society is very useful for explaining why Marxists see the family as shaped by the interests of the ruling class.

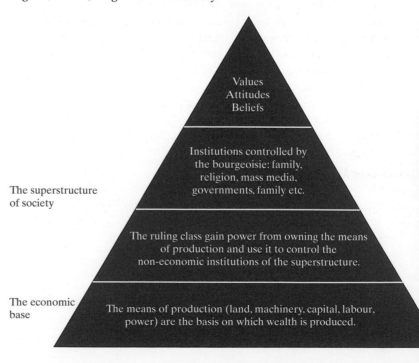

The superstructure of society

The economic base

Fig 8
Marxist model of society

Values
Attitudes
Beliefs

Institutions controlled by the bourgeoisie: family, religion, mass media, governments, family etc.

The ruling class gain power from owning the means of production and use it to control the non-economic institutions of the superstructure.

The means of production (land, machinery, capital, labour, power) are the basis on which wealth is produced.

Marxist perspectives on the family

- Frederick Engels (1884) argued that the family developed so that men could be certain of the paternity of children, with marriage allowing them to control women's sexuality. This enabled them to be more confident that they were passing their property down to their biological offspring.
- Eli Zaretsky (1976) sees the family as a prop to the capitalist system. The unpaid **domestic labour** of housewives reproduces future generations of workers at no cost to capitalist employers. The family consumes the commodities produced by capitalist companies, helping the bourgeoisie to make profits. It also provides comfort to **alienated** workers, enabling them to carry on working.
- Nicos Poulantzas (1969) sees the family as part of the superstructure of society. He describes it as part of the ideological state apparatus which is controlled by the bourgeoisie and used to create values, attitudes and beliefs which support the capitalist system and the position of the ruling class.
- The view of Poulantzas was supported by David Cooper (1972), who sees the family as 'an ideological conditioning device' in which children learn to conform to authority so they will become cooperative and easily exploited workers.

Criticisms of Marxism

The Marxist view of the family has been criticized from a variety of viewpoints:

- Some modern evidence contradicts the view that the family only developed after the herding of animals was introduced.
- Zaretsky has been criticized for exaggerating the extent to which the family can be an escape from alienating work since the family can also be characterized by cruelty, neglect and violence.
- Some families are anti-capitalist and socialize their children into beliefs which are critical of the ruling class.
- **Feminists** criticize Marxists for neglecting the exploitation of women; **postmodernists** criticize them for ignoring the variety of family types present in society today; and functionalists believe that Marxists ignore the beneficial functions of the family for society.

Strengths of Marxism

Marxism is useful for highlighting the importance of economic influences on family life and because it raises the possibility that the family as an institution benefits some social groups (higher classes) more than others.

Examiners' notes

Remember that Marxist-feminist views (see page 30) of the family are very closely linked to Marxist views.

Examiners' notes

You are quite likely to need to compare Marxism with other theories in 33-mark questions.

Feminist theories of the family

The basic principles of feminism

There are several different types of feminist theory, but all of them share certain beliefs in common:

- There is a fundamental division in society between men and women.
- Women are to some extent exploited by men.
- Society is male-dominated or **patriarchal**. (Literally, patriarchal means 'rule by the father', but it is used by feminists to indicate that men have more power than women and the interests of men largely shape how societies run.)
- A critical approach to existing sociology, arguing that it has a pro-male bias. Feminists call male-dominated sociology '**malestream**' sociology, claiming that most sociology is written by men, about men and for men. For example, most early studies of the family used all-male samples and paid little attention to women's roles and work within the family such as the role of mother and the work of mothering or housework.

From the early 1970s, feminist thinking became more influential in sociology and this was reflected in a growing number of studies of the family from a feminist viewpoint. However, there are important differences between the perspectives of different feminists.

The table below summarizes three of the main varieties of feminism that have been applied to the study of the family.

	Radical feminism	Marxist feminism	Liberal feminism
Society is controlled by:	Men	Men and capitalists (the wealthy ruling class)	Largely by men who have more power than women, but women do have some power.
Society is defined as:	Patriarchal (male dominated)	Patriarchal	Basically democratic but it is also sexist with discrimination against women.
Who benefits from inequalities in society?	Men	Men in general, but ruling-class men in particular. Working-class men get wives to work for them (e.g. housework) but the ruling class exploit women both as workers and wives.	Nobody. Gender stereotypes mean that men miss out on the private side of life (e.g. raising children) and women miss out on public life (e.g. paid employment).

Examiners' notes

All answers on feminism should use the concept of patriarchy.

Examiners' notes

By including different types of feminism in your answer you will tend to get into higher mark bands because you are displaying a wide range of knowledge and understanding of theories. In 33-mark questions specifically about feminism, be sure to include several feminist perspectives.

	Radical feminism	Marxist feminism	Liberal feminism
Main ideas behind the theory:	Women are dominated by men due to biology (women give birth, men are stronger) and use violence, or **ideology** (distorted beliefs).	Men's financial power keeps women in their place. Women do more unpaid work (e.g. as mothers and housewives) and receive lower wages, making them financially dependent on men.	Socialization into gender roles (e.g. differences in boys' and girls' toys) and sexist discrimination (e.g. in the labour market), restrict women's opportunities.
Solutions to the exploitation of women:	Radical change (e.g. a female-dominated society or separation of the sexes).	Communist revolution or more economic equality to get rid of men's financial power.	Gradual reform. Getting rid of sexism in socialization (e.g. children's books) and the use of language. Laws against discrimination (e.g. Equal Pay Act).
Criticisms:	The idea of patriarchy is too broad and doesn't really explain why women are exploited. It exaggerates the extent of inequality and fails to take account of the development of greater equality.	Places too much emphasis on economic factors.	Lacks a theory of the underlying causes of inequality.

Table 4
Main varieties of feminism

Difference feminism

The three feminist perspectives outlined above all tend to see women as a single group who share interests and are all equally exploited. However, difference feminism emphasizes that women are not one single united group but rather have a variety of interests.

Black feminists, for example, stress the importance of racial/ethnic differences between women, while other difference feminists emphasize differences in class, age or nationality. Difference feminists point out that not all women are equally exploited.

Examiners' notes

If an exam question asks you about Marxist theories of the family, remember that you can include Marxist feminism in your answer as well as conventional Marxism.

Examiners' notes

Remember that the different perspectives can be used to criticize and evaluate one another.

Essential notes

Another criticism that has been made of all these varieties of feminism is that the concept of patriarchy does not really explain gender inequality, but only describes it.

Examiners' notes

Difference feminism has much in common with postmodernism, and commenting on this could help you demonstrate greater theoretical depth in essay questions.

Essential notes

Evidence of domestic violence and sexual abuse perpetrated by men can also be used to support radical feminism. This is discussed on page 61.

Examiners' notes

There are a number of ideas in these notes which can also be used to answer questions on roles, responsibilities and relationships, which is the subject of pp 56-65.

Essential notes

Some studies in the sections on conjugal roles and power in households (page 58) can be used to support Marxist feminist views.

Feminist perspectives and the family

Radical feminism and the family

Radical feminists believe that the family plays a major role in maintaining the oppression of women in a patriarchal, male-dominated society.

Germaine Greer (2000) argues that even in marriage today women remain subservient to their husbands. She believes that single women are generally happier than married women and this is reflected in the high number of divorces instigated by women. Greer claims that wives are much more likely to suffer physical and sexual abuse than husbands, and daughters are often victims of sexual abuse by male relatives within the family.

Marxist feminism and the family

Marxist feminists believe that the family benefits the capitalist system and in doing so exploits women.

- Margaret Benston (1972) claims that wives are used to produce and rear cheap labour for employers. The childcare they do is unpaid, and they also help to maintain their husbands as workers at no cost to employers.
- Fran Ansley (1972) believes that wives suffer as a result of the frustration experienced by their husbands in the **alienating** work that they do for capitalists.

Liberal feminism and the family

The liberal feminist Jennifer Somerville (2000) believes that women are still disadvantaged in families, but she criticizes radical and Marxist feminists for failing to accept that progress has been made in some ways:

- Women now have much more choice about whether to marry, whether they take paid work when married, and whether they stay married.
- There is now greater equality within marriage and greater sharing of the responsibility for paid and unpaid work and childcare.
- Most women still value relationships with men.

However, she agrees there are still inequalities within marriage that need to be tackled through pragmatic reform. For example, better childcare is needed for working parents, and more flexibility is needed in jobs so that both men and women can contribute fully to family life.

Criticisms of radical, Marxist and liberal feminist perspectives on the family

All these perspectives have been criticized for:

- exaggerating the exploitation of women within the family
- largely failing to acknowledge the increasing equality between men and women
- oversimplifying by taking little account of differences in the circumstances of different groups of women
- ignoring examples where men are victims of abuse in families
- in particular, not taking account of class, ethnic and age differences.

Functionalists criticize feminists for failing to acknowledge the positive contribution of the family to society.

Postmodernists criticize feminists for failing to acknowledge the extent to which society and family life have changed.

Difference feminism and the family

This perspective recognizes that there is increasing family diversity today and women may not be equally exploited in all family types. For example, many women are lone parents and as such cannot be exploited by a cohabiting man. There are also differences in gender relationships in families from different ethnic backgrounds.

- Linda Nicholson (1997) believes that women are often better off outside traditional families, and all types of family and household should be socially accepted because they suit women in different circumstances.
- Cheshire Calhoun (1997) points out that women cannot be exploited by men in lesbian families. She believes that there is increasing choice in family life, and gay and lesbian families are examples of 'chosen families'.

Criticisms of difference feminism

Difference feminism is not as easy to criticize as other forms of feminism because it recognizes differences in family life. However, other types of feminists criticize it for losing sight of continuing inequalities between men and women within the family.

The contribution of feminism to understanding the family

Despite the criticisms of feminism, it has contributed to the sociology of the family in a number of ways:

- showing that the family may benefit some members, particularly adult males, more than others
- highlighting the existence of violence, abuse and exploitation within the family
- conducting research into areas of family life that have either been neglected or not been studied before. These include conjugal roles, motherhood, pregnancy, childbirth and childcare
- analyzing the contribution of housework to the economy
- helping to correct the masculine bias in the previous sociology of the family and to illuminate family life from the perspective of women.

Examiners' notes

You can develop these criticisms in more detail by discussing in depth how feminism differs from functionalist, Marxist and postmodern theories.

Examiners' notes

Studies of the growth of gay and lesbian families are very useful for answering a wide range of questions about the family, including those on increasing diversity and roles and relationships.

Examiners' notes

The highest marks for evaluation tend to be given to those who have a balanced discussion – that is, they look at both the strengths and weaknesses of a perspective approach or study, especially in the longer 33-mark questions.

A comparison of theories of the family

Types of theory
Sociological theories can be divided into a number of types.

Macro and micro theories
1. **Macro theories** examine society as a whole, so that they look at the big picture.
2. **Micro theories** are on a smaller scale and look at parts of society and small social groups. They tend not to relate the small-scale studies to the bigger picture of society as a whole in any detail.

Structural and social action theories
3. **Structural theories** examine the way society as a whole fits together. They try to uncover the main features of society that determine its overall shape.
4. **Social action theories** look at small-scale interaction; for example, looking at interaction in classrooms or within families.

Not surprisingly, structural theories also tend to be macro theories, and social action theories also tend to be micro theories.

Consensus versus conflict
Another way of dividing up theories is in terms of whether they emphasize consensus or conflict.

Consensus theories stress shared culture and shared interests within society and tend to assume that society usually works smoothly.

Conflict theories emphasize that there are sources of disagreement and disharmony in society based upon differences in interest. What is good for one group in society tends to be bad for another group in society. For example, men may benefit at the expense of women, the ruling class at the expense of the subject class or the ethnic majority at the expense of ethnic minorities. These differences of interest can lead to conflicts of a variety of forms including arguments, violence, crime, strikes, riots or war.

Functionalism, Marxism and feminism as types of theory
The table below summarizes the main differences between these three key theories in terms of the above criteria.

Examiners' notes

It is essential to include these terms where appropriate in any 33-mark questions asking you to evaluate a sociological theory.

Examiners' notes

This table provides a useful framework for questions asking you to evaluate any of these theories. Remember to include theories when you evaluate the issue in a question. This will increase your marks for analysis and evaluation.

Theory	Functionalism	Marxism	Feminism
Macro or Micro?	Macro – looks at how the basic needs of society as a whole are met.	Macro – looks at social classes in society as a whole.	Macro – examines the overall power of men in society, but some feminists focus on the micro (e.g. looking at domestic violence).
Structural or social action?	Structural – examines how the main institutions of society fit together and meet basic needs.	Structural – examines the relationship between the economic base and superstructure of society.	Structural – examines patriarchy as a structure in society, but some feminists concentrate on interaction (e.g. between husbands and wives).

Consensus or conflict?	Consensus – achieved through shared values and norms produced through socialization.	Conflict – based upon class differences between ruling class and subject class.	Conflict – based upon gender; the exploitation of women by men leads to conflict within the home and in the wider society.

Table 5
Main differences between functionalism, Marxism and feminism

Functionalist, Marxist and feminist views on the family

The general features of these three perspectives are reflected in their views on the family.

Functionalist view of the family

- The family meets functional prerequisites including sexual, reproductive, economic and emotional needs.
- It has moved towards the isolated nuclear family to facilitate geographical mobility in industrial society.
- Traditional gender roles continue and are functional for society.
- This view identifies and explains the positive benefits of family life, but can be over-optimistic, ignoring the 'dark' side of family life.

Marxist view of the family

- The family acts as an ideological state apparatus, legitimizing and stabilizing the capitalist system.
- The nuclear family continues to dominate, playing an increasing role in consumption.
- Relationships are hierarchical and male-dominated, based on economic control, just as the ruling class dominates society.
- This view analyzes how economic inequality might shape family life, but places too much emphasis on economic factors and not enough on gender differences. Ignores positive benefits of family for society.

Feminist view of the family

- The family is a patriarchal institution maintaining male power and dominance.
- Radical feminists believe the patriarchal nuclear family dominates, but postmodern and difference feminists are more aware of increasing diversity.
- Patriarchal dominance continues, but liberal feminists accept some move towards equality.
- This view introduces the study of neglected aspects of family life and has contributed to the understanding of family relationships, but it emphasizes gender inequality to the exclusion of other inequalities. Radical feminists do not acknowledge improvements in women's position.

Conclusion

All these theories have a certain amount in common in that all have a model of society as a whole and a sense of its structure, but functionalism is a consensus theory while Marxism and feminism are conflict theories. There is more variety within feminism, which has a less developed model of the structure of society than the other two perspectives.

Examiners' notes

The individual sections on each of these theories provide you with more details. You will need a fair amount of descriptive detail to pick up all the knowledge and understanding marks if you are asked to outline and evaluate a particular perspective.

Examiners' notes

Answers should be balanced, looking at both similarities and differences, and strengths and weaknesses. Extra marks can be gained by using other theories to analyze and evaluate. As well as those included here you might also be able to use the theories of the New Right and/or postmodernism.

The growth of family diversity

What is family diversity?

The idea of **family diversity** suggests that in any one era, no particular type of family is dominant or can be considered the norm. A good deal of historical research on the family has sought to identify the typical family type in different eras. For example, research has examined whether the **nuclear family** is the typical or dominant type in industrial societies.

Some historians, such as Michael Anderson (1980), have argued that there has always been diversity in family types, but most sociologists of the family before the 1980s assumed that family diversity was not the norm. More recently some sociologists have continued to argue that a single family type is dominant. For example, Peter Willmott (1988) believes that the **dispersed extended family** is the norm.

The idea that a single family type is dominant is also found in media images. According to Ann Oakley (1982), marketing and advertising often uses what it sees as a typical family to sell products. She discusses how these media present the conventional family as 'nuclear families composed of legally married couples, voluntarily choosing the parenthood of one or more (but not too many) children'. Edmund Leach (1967) described this as the **cereal packet image of the family**. There is a strong **ideology** supporting this family type as the best type of family (see page 6).

The idea of family diversity, however, suggests this stereotype of the nuclear family is highly misleading and outdated. The argument that diversity or variation in families is normal has been developed by a number of sociologists.

Family diversity in the UK

Robert and Rhona Rapoport (1982) were the first British sociologists to point out that nuclear family households have become a minority in Britain. Since they first wrote about diversity, nuclear families have continued to become a smaller proportion of all households in the UK.

In Table 6 the categories 'family household with 1–2 and 3 or more dependent children' represent the nuclear family. This shows that, in 1971, 35% of households were of this type, but by 2008 only 21% were.

Examiners' notes

You need to be prepared for a wide variety of questions on this topic including 33-mark questions about the extent of diversity, and 17-mark questions about reasons for particular types of diversity.

	1971	1981	1991	2001	2008
One-person households					
Under state pension age	6%	8%	11%	14%	15%
Over state pension age	12%	14%	16%	15%	15%
One-family households					
Couple:					
No children	27%	26%	28%	29%	29%
1–2 dependent children	26%	25%	20%	19%	18%
3 or more dependent children	9%	6%	5%	4%	3%

	1971	1981	1991	2001	2008
Non-dependent children only	8%	8%	8%	6%	6%
Lone parent:					
Dependent children	3%	5%	6%	7%	7%
Non-dependent children only	4%	4%	4%	3%	3%
Two or more unrelated adults	4%	5%	3%	3%	3%
Multi-family households	1%	1%	1%	1%	1%

Table 6
UK households: by type of household and family

The most significant increases are in the percentage of households consisting of one person under or over state pension age and lone parents with dependent children.

Household types increasing 1971–2008	One-person households under state pension age
	One-person households over state pension age
	Couple-only households
	Lone-parent households with dependent children
	Lone-parent households with non-dependent children
Family types decreasing 1971–2008	One-family households with 1–2 dependent children
	One-family households with three or more dependent children
	One-family households with non-dependent children
	Households with two or more unrelated adults

Table 7
Growing and declining household types, 1971–2008

These changes represent an increase in the proportion of households with a structure other than that of the nuclear family. Overall, there is a more even spread across the various diverse family structures.

Types of diversity

The Rapoports (1982) identify five main types of diversity:

1. **Organizational diversity.** This involves variations in family structure, household type, kinship network and the **division of labour** within the home. Examples include **lone-parent families**, **dual-earner families**, **cohabiting** couples and **reconstituted families** (families formed out of the fragments of previous families after a divorce). Reconstituted families can include stepchildren, half-brothers and sisters and so on.
2. **Cultural diversity**. This refers to differences in lifestyles between families of different ethnic, national or religious backgrounds. For example, differences between British Asian and white British families, British and Polish families, Catholic and Protestant families.

Essential notes

To give a rounded answer to questions about family diversity you will also need to look at the next pages which include some alternative interpretations of the trends shown in these statistics. Not everybody agrees that the figures show a marked decline in nuclear families.

☞ This topic continues on the next two pages

Examiners' notes

It is important to learn and remember these different types of diversity in order to answer questions on this topic. You can also add the new types of diversity discussed at the end of this section.

Essential notes

The most useful theoretical explanations of increasing diversity are put forward by sociologists of modernity, such as Anthony Giddens and Ulrich Beck, and sociologists of postmodernity such as Judith Stacey (see page 48). All of them relate the changes to social trends which break up traditional patterns of family life, although their exact explanations vary.

Examiners' notes

To further explain why some of these changes are taking place, use material on increasing divorce rates and cohabitation on pages 17-18.

3. **Class diversity**. There are also differences in families of **upper-class**, **middle-class** and **working-class** origin. These might include relationships between adults and the way children are socialized.
4. Stage in the **life-cycle.** For example, there are differences between newly married couples without children, couples with dependent children and families with non-dependent children.
5. **Cohort diversity.** A **cohort** is a group of people born over the same period of time (for example, the baby boomer generation born in the period 1946 to 1964). This generation is sometimes seen as having a different pattern of family life than their parents' generation, for example in having more dual-earner families.

There is further discussion of many of these types of diversity in subsequent sections.

Reasons for diversification

Graham Allen and Graham Crow (2001) believe that since the Rapoports were writing diversification has continued. There is no longer a fixed set of stages in the life cycle and each family follows a more unpredictable course complicated by cohabitation, **divorce**, remarriage, and so on. This reflects greater individual choice and 'the increasing separation of sex, marriage and parenthood'.

They give the following reasons for increasing diversity:

- A rising **divorce rate** caused by factors such as changes in the divorce law, rising social acceptance of divorce and greater independence for women.
- An increase in **lone-parent households**, partly resulting from increasing divorce, but also from greater acceptance of births outside marriage.
- **Cohabitation** becoming increasingly acceptable, partly as a result of the decline in the influence of religion (secularization).
- Declining marriage rates as people marry later and an increasing minority choose not to marry at all.
- The rise in the number of **stepfamilies** as a result of increasing divorce.
- The formation of more **reconstituted families** owing to the number of people remarrying (a quarter of marriages are remarriages).

New types of diversity

Over recent decades new types of diversity in addition to those identified by the Rapoports have developed as a result of liberalization in attitudes to sexuality and the introduction of **new reproductive technologies**.

Sexual diversity

Jeffery Weeks, Brian Heaphey and Catherine Donovan (1999) see the increase in openly **gay and lesbian households** and families as contributing to the increase in diversity. They believe that gay men and lesbians often see their households and even their friendship networks as being **chosen families**. On the basis of this they argue that an important social change is taking place in which whom we see to be part of our family is more important than ties of blood or marriage. **Friendship networks** can now function as if they were families. This is part of a general move towards a greater emphasis on individual choice rather than the duties and obligations of family life.

- Sasha Roseneil (2005) links the development of chosen families to the breakdown of the **heteronorm** – the belief that all intimate relationships should be based on heterosexuality. TV programmes such as *Friends* and *Will and Grace* highlight the possibility that there are alternative networks to traditional families.
- The Civil Partnerships Act of 2004 in the UK recognized and legitimized gay and lesbian relationships.

New reproductive technologies

New reproductive technologies date from 1978 when the first 'test-tube baby', Louise Brown, was born through in-vitro fertilization.

Surrogate motherhood, where one woman carries a foetus produced by the egg of another woman, is now possible. This raises questions about who the parents of the child are since the **birth parents** and the **genetic parents** are different. It adds to the complexity of possible family types and has even led to a grandmother giving birth to her own grandchild.

The beanpole family

Further types of **diversity** involve other variations on the traditional nuclear family, including the **beanpole family** (see p 9) as defined by Julia Brannen (2003). This has weak **intragenerational** ties (within generations, for example, between brothers, sisters and cousins) but stronger **intergenerational** ties (between parents, children, grandparents and grandchildren).

The reasons for the weakness of intragenerational ties include:

- higher rates of **geographical mobility** as more people live further from other family members
- falling family size so that people have fewer siblings
- increasing family breakdown, which can lead to the severing of ties with in-laws.

Stronger intergenerational ties may be caused by:

- greater longevity so that children are more likely to have living grandparents
- an increase in elderly parents requiring care from their children, in part owing to greater longevity but also impacted by limited provision of state support for the elderly
- an increase in thc proportion of dual-earner families where working parents ask grandparents to help more with childcare
- a rise in the proportion of lone-parent families where mothers or fathers get more help from their parents.

Essential notes

The idea of chosen families is extremely useful in answering a wide range of questions. It challenges conventional definitions of the family since it means that families are no longer based on kinship or marriage and it can therefore be used to question most of the theories of the family. It does, however, fit with the postmodern view of the family which sees traditional assumptions about the family as no longer being accepted.

Diversity and the decline of conventional families

The implications of family diversity

Some researchers see increasing **diversity** as not only a decline of the **nuclear family** but also as undermining this institution as a model of a normal or conventional family. The following key study backs up this view.

Examiners' notes

This is a useful study which can be used to answer questions on a wide range of topics including key trends in ethnicity and diversity, as well as general questions on family diversity. You will be awarded higher marks for quoting specific studies to back up or to criticize theories or to illustrate trends.

Key study

Geoff Dench, Kate Gavron and Michael Young (2006) carried out a study in Bethnal Green in the 1990s to follow up Michael Young and Peter Willmott's study of the area from the 1950s (see page 8). They found that earlier family patterns where working-class residents lived in nuclear families with strong kinship links had largely disappeared. This had been replaced by a new **individualism** in which **cohabitation**, **divorce**, **separation** and lone parenthood were all more common. Only the local Bangladeshi population had a dominant pattern of conventional family life based upon marriage and the male **breadwinner**.

Such research has led commentators such as Brenda Almond (2006) to claim that the family is **fragmenting** (breaking into pieces) and is more concerned with the needs of adult members than creating a stable unit in which children can be raised.

Chester – the neo-conventional family

The widespread view that the nuclear family is threatened by diversity and is breaking up, or even disappearing, has been challenged by Robert Chester (1985). He found that the following main features of family life have remained fairly stable since the Second World War:

- Most people still get married.
- Most children are reared by their natural parents.
- Most people live in a household headed by a married couple.
- Most people stay married.

Although the situation has changed since Chester was writing, most of the above is still true. (Although the proportion of marriages ending in divorce is now approaching 50%.)

Chester argued that the statistics used to support the idea of increasing diversity can be misleading. They are usually based upon the proportion of households of different types and not the proportion of people living in different types of household. This makes a significant difference because nuclear family households tend to be larger than other households since by definition they contain at least two adults and one child. Table 8 shows the percentage of the population living in different household types.

Examiners' notes

Chester's views can be used to balance the ideas of those who believe in increasing diversity. You are more likely to get into the top mark bands for analysis and evaluation in 33-mark questions if you can balance the competing viewpoints

Percentages	1971	1981	1991	2001	2008
One-person households	6%	8%	11%	12%	12%
One-family households					
Couple:					
No children	19%	20%	23%	25%	25%
Dependent children	52%	47%	41%	38%	36%
Non-dependent children only	10%	10%	11%	9%	9%
Lone parent	4%	6%	10%	11%	11%
Other households	9%	9%	4%	5%	6%
All people in private households (=100%)	53.4%	53.9%	54.1%	56.7%	58.8%

Table 8
People in UK households: by type of household and family

In 2008, 70% of people were still living in households headed by a couple. This represented a fall from 81% in 1971, but was still a large majority of the population. Not all of these families were nuclear families in the sense of including both parents and dependent children but, as Chester pointed out, couples without dependent children often go on to have children later. Furthermore some one-person households consist of widows and widowers who were once married but whose children have now grown up. Chester concluded that most people still live in nuclear families for much of their lives.

Chester did believe that one major change had taken place in the life of nuclear families, a change in the roles of husband and wife. He accepted that married women are increasingly employed outside the home and he called this type of family, in which both parents have paid employment, the **neo-conventional family**.

Conclusion

Elizabeth Silva and Carol Smart (1999) agree with Chester that cohabiting or married couples, many of whom have children or go on to have children, remain very important in contemporary family life.

Jennifer Somerville (2000) agrees that the decline in traditional families can be exaggerated, but also emphasizes that there are important changes taking place. These include:

- Sex outside marriage becoming common.
- More couples who choose not to have children.
- Increasing numbers of lone parents.
- Greater diversity as a result of variations in the family life of different **ethnic groups**.

Essential notes

These views offer some support to those who have tried to identify a single dominant family type in the UK such as Peter Willmott (see page 9).

Cultural diversity

Religious and ethnic diversity

Cultural diversity concerns diversity in family types that results from differences in lifestyle or culture. A number of factors can affect culture, including **social class** and sexuality, but this section examines differences based on religion and ethnicity.

Religious and **ethnic diversity** are closely linked since one important difference between ethnic groups can be their religion. For example, followers of the Sikh religion are likely to be part of Indian ethnic groups, while many Muslims belong to Pakistani or Bangladeshi ethnic groups.

Religion can have an influence on family life in its own right; for example, it can affect the likelihood of marriage and having dependent children. The 2001 census found that in the UK Muslims were the most likely group to live in **households** with dependent children, followed by Sikhs, Hindus and Buddhists, with Christians and Jews least likely to live in such households.

Religious beliefs can affect family size. For example, the disapproval of contraception by the Roman Catholic Church may explain the higher average family size amongst Roman Catholics than Protestants.

Ethnicity and diversity

- **Ethnic groups** are groups within a population regarded by themselves or others as culturally distinctive; they usually see themselves as sharing a common origin. Ethnicity may be linked to religion, nationality and other aspects of culture such as language and lifestyle.
- Largely as a result of **migration**, the UK has a number of distinctive ethnic groups. The largest minority ethnic groups in the UK are those of South Asian or African-Caribbean origin. The Irish and Chinese can also be regarded as minority ethnic groups.
- Minority ethnic groups can be seen as adding to the diversity of family types in the UK to the extent that they have distinctive family patterns or lifestyles. However, if their family life has become very similar to that of the white British majority, minority ethnic groups may not contribute to the diversity.

The extent of ethnic diversity

The 2001 census found significant differences in the family life of ethnic groups in the UK. For example:

- In 2001, 8% of white and 7% of Black-Caribbean households were headed by an unmarried, **cohabiting** couple compared with just 2% of British Asian households.
- 23% of Black-Caribbean households were **lone-parent families** compared with 8% of Indian and 9% of white British households.
- Black-Caribbean lone parents are much more likely to be single (71%) than Bangladeshi lone parents (5%).
- In 2001, 71% of Black-Caribbean adults were single (never married) compared with 39% of white British people, but just 8% of Pakistanis and 5% of Bangladeshis.

Examiners' notes

Be prepared to answer individual questions on ethnicity and family life and also to integrate material on this topic into general questions about diversity.

	One-person households	Pensioner families	Married couple families	Cohabiting couple families	Lone-parent families	Other households
White British	31	9	37	8	9	6
Indian	15	3	53	2	8	19
Pakistani	12	1	51	2	11	23
Bangladeshi	9	1	54	2	11	24
Black-Caribbean	38	3	19	7	23	9
Chinese	28	2	41	4	8	16
All households	30	9	37	8	10	7

Table 9
Household type by ethnic group (figures are percentages)

Asian families

Research by Ghazala Bhatti (1999) using in-depth interviews of Asian families in southern England found a strong emphasis on family loyalty and on trying to maintain traditional family practices. Izzat, the principle of family honour, was taken very seriously, and mothers saw their family roles as the most important duty in life. Fathers usually took on the traditional **breadwinner** role. This evidence suggests that Asian families add to diversity by maintaining traditional, **nuclear families** but with very strong **extended kinship networks** and a strong sense of mutual obligation.

However, there was some evidence that life in the UK has begun to erode the distinctiveness of Asian families, with increasing numbers of clashes between younger and older generations. In some families children rebelled against traditional values, for example, by seeking to marry outside their own community against parental wishes.

African-Caribbean families

The Policy Studies Institute (1997) found that British African-Caribbean households had fewer long-term partnerships than other groups, were more likely to have children outside marriage, and had above average rates of **divorce** and **separation**.

Research by Mary Chamberlain (1999) has found that brothers, sisters, uncles and aunts have more importance in African-Caribbean families than in white British families. Siblings often play a significant part in bringing up younger brothers and sisters, and women are quite likely to assist sisters in bringing up children.

Tracey Reynolds (2002) argues that despite the large number of female-headed households amongst Black-Caribbean families in the UK, in reality, diversity is the main characteristic of family life in this group. As well as conventional nuclear families and female-headed families, **visiting relationships** are also common where the female head of household has a male partner who visits her frequently but does not live under the same roof.

Conclusion

The evidence suggests that ethnic minorities do continue to add to the diversity of family life, though convergence with the family life of white British families has occurred to a limited degree.

Examiners' notes

You can get additional marks by showing that you are aware of differences between specific ethnic groups. For example, amongst South Asians there are significant differences, with considerably higher rates of one-person households amongst Indians (15%) than Bangladeshis (9%).

Examiners' notes

Markers will be looking to see if you have compared patterns of family life in ethnic minorities with majority, white British patterns, and if you have demonstrated an awareness of changes over time. Use studies to indicate whether the family life of different ethnic groups is becoming more similar.

Essential notes

Some sociologists have claimed that there is a distinctive family type among the black population of the Caribbean and the Americas dominated by mothers who are lone parents but get support from other female relatives. Chamberlain's study provides some evidence that this family type has been imported to the UK.

Family diversity and lone parenthood

The growth of lone parenthood

The section on trends in parenting (page 22) showed that in the UK between 1971 and 2008 the percentage of lone-parent family households increased from 3% to 7%. This section examines the reasons for the growth and the effects of lone parenthood in more detail.

Demographic causes of lone parenthood

Graham Allan and Graham Crow (2001) explain the increase in lone parenthood in terms of two factors:

- An increase in **marital breakdown** (particularly divorce).
- A rise in births to unmarried mothers.

They suggest that both these trends can be explained in terms of an increasing acceptance of **diversity** and choice in family life. (See page 18 for explanations of rising divorce.)

David Morgan (1994) sees changing relationships between men and women as important, with greater equality between the sexes making it more feasible for women to bring up children on their own. In addition, more employment opportunities for women encourage them to have a life in which they are not dependent upon a male partner.

Changing attitudes and lone parenthood

Evidence from the British Social Attitudes Survey (2001) shows that younger age groups are much more accepting of parenthood outside marriage. It is no longer regarded as necessary for an unmarried couple to legitimize a birth by having a 'shotgun wedding' before a child is born. David Morgan (1994) notes that much less stigma is now attached to **illegitimacy**. However, research by Louie Burghes and Mark Brown (1995) suggests that most lone parents do not regard the situation as ideal, and the British Social Attitudes Survey (2001) found there is still disapproval of teenage pregnancies.

Dependency culture

According to Charles Murray (1999), the increase in lone parenthood is a result of an over-generous welfare system which makes it possible for lone parents to live on benefits with housing provided by the state. Murray sees lone parents as part of a welfare-dependent **underclass**. Murray's views have been strongly criticized for being based on limited research.

Allan and Crow point out that most lone mothers find a new partner within a few years and do not rely upon benefits throughout their offspring's childhood. This view is supported by research from the Department for Work and Pensions (2004).

The effects of lone parenthood

Research suggests that lone parenthood can lead to a range of negative consequences, particularly for the children. These include:

- A greater chance of living in **poverty**. For example, in 2005, 41% of lone-parent families had a household income of less than £200 per week, compared with 8% of married couples with children, and

---

Examiners' notes

A typical 17-mark question might ask you to identify and explain two reasons for the increase in lone parenthood. Remember that one way of reaching the 13- to 17-mark band is to include recent evidence, as well as theories and/or concepts.

Examiners' notes

Charles Murray is associated with the theory of the New Right (see page 52). This perspective can be criticized using other theories, particularly feminism and postmodernism. Incorporating criticisms from competing theoretical perspectives helps to get you into the top mark band.

11% of cohabiting couples. Research from the Joseph Rowntree Foundation (1999) found that children from lone-parent families were more than four times as likely to worry about having too little income as children from two-parent families. However, not all lone parents are poor – some have very high incomes – so the experience of children varies considerably.

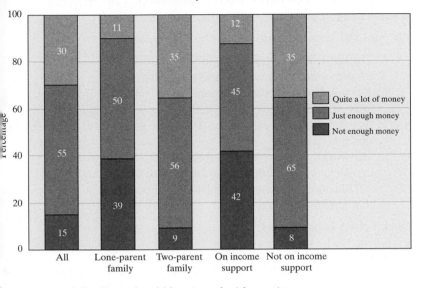

Fig 9
Children's opinions of income adequacy (Joseph Rowntree Foundation, 1999)

However, such findings should be viewed with caution.

- Research suggests that any negative effects are more the result of low income than the lack of two parents.
- Research by Louie Burghes (1996) found that the negative educational effects on children in families where lone parenthood was the result of divorce had started before the divorce, suggesting that family instability rather than lone parenthood was responsible.
- E. E. Cashmore (1985) points out that having one parent may even be better for children than having two parents if the absent parent is abusive or violent.
- Sara Arber (2000) found that whilst the children of unemployed lone parents had more ill-health on average than other children, their health was no worse than other groups if their parent was in employment.

Conclusion

Lone parenthood undoubtedly adds to the diversity of family life in the UK. However, few lone parents bring up children on their own out of choice and many find a new partner or would like to do so.

As David Morgan (1994) concludes, there are probably some negative effects overall of lone parenthood but most of the apparent harmful effects are the result of low income or other factors.

Essential notes

Many studies that claim there are negative effects of lone parenthood for children can be criticized on methodological grounds. Most use small samples and fail to control for the effects of low income on outcomes for children. More sophisticated research does control for the effects of low income/poverty.

Social class and diversity

Social class

Another source of diversity in family life is **social class**. Social classes can be defined in a number of ways, but all definitions are based upon the idea that groups in society can be divided according to their economic circumstances. For example, income, wealth and job are frequently seen as the most important factors distinguishing social classes.

On this basis, three main classes can be distinguished:

1. The **upper class**, who own significant amounts of wealth, for example, land, property, businesses or shares.
2. The **middle class**, who have non-manual jobs (that is, their jobs primarily involve mental rather than physical labour) with relatively high pay and job security. They usually have higher-level qualifications.
3. The **working class**, who have manual jobs (their jobs primarily involve physical labour). They do not usually have higher-level qualifications and on average have lower pay and less job security than the middle class.

Social class subcultures

Early research by sociologists such as David Lockwood (1966) claimed to have identified distinctive **class subcultures** associated with the middle class and the working class. Some of the main features of these subcultures are outlined in Table 10.

Table 10
Social class subcultures

	Working class	Middle class
Time orientation	Present-time orientation	Future-time orientation
Attitude to gratification	Seek immediate gratification	Deferred gratification
Collectivism versus individualism	Success achieved through collective action	Success achieved through individual action
Attitudes to luck	Chances in life based on luck or fate	Chances in life based on ability and hard work

It is debatable how far these class subcultures still exist today, but some sociologists have argued that there are still differences in social class subcultures and that these might affect family life. For example, the working class may be more likely to have strong **extended families** because of their positive attitude towards collectivism, while the middle class might put more emphasis on promoting the individual achievement of their children, and could therefore be more **child-centred**.

Although these suggestions are generalizations and there are obviously likely to be variations between individual families, research has examined whether there are significant differences between middle-class and working-class families.

Examiners' notes

You will need to demonstrate a basic understanding of class differences and be able to go into detail about the different classes to answer questions on class diversity.

Examiners' notes

You can gain evaluation marks by pointing out that these descriptions of class subcultures are rather dated and may now be stereotypical. However, they may still be relevant because they continue to be applied to explain class differences in family life.

Statistical research on class differences

In a review of research, Ivan Reid (1999) identified the following differences between the family life of the middle and the working class.

- The working class are likely to marry earlier than the middle class.
- Divorce rates are higher in working-class families than in middle-class families.
- In the middle class, husbands are more likely than wives to remarry, whereas in the working class, wives are more likely to remarry than husbands.
- Working-class women are more likely to have children at an early age, whereas in the middle class age at first birth is on average later.

In most cases the statistical differences are quite small and vary greatly.

Family structure

Much early research on the family such as that by Peter Willmott and Michael Young (1973) found stronger **extended kinship networks** in working-class communities than amongst the middle class. The middle class tended to be more **geographically mobile**, meaning that they tended to live further from their **kin**, whereas members of working-class communities were more likely to live close together.

Recent research by Geoff Dench, Kate Gavron and Michael Young (2006) conducted in the predominantly working-class East End of London found only a few white, working-class families with strong kinship networks remained. They found considerable diversity of relationships within working-class households, for example, 21% were living in **single-person households**. According to these researchers, diversity is now characteristic of both working-class and middle-class families, based on a new **individualism** in which individuals construct the family life that suits their own particular circumstances.

Child-rearing practices

Some sociologists argue that middle-class families are more child-centred and are more concerned with the long-term well-being of their children. For example, Leon Feinstein (2003) used data from the British Cohort Study which suggested that working-class parents show less interest in their children's education than middle-class parents.

However, Blackstone and Mortimore (1994) argue that working-class parents are just as interested in their children's education as middle-class parents, but it is more difficult for them to take an active role in supporting their children because they have less knowledge of the educational system, fewer educational qualifications themselves, less in common with middle-class teachers and are often short of time owing to long working hours.

Sociologists such as Pierre Bourdieu (1984) believe that cultural differences between classes are the result of material inequality, which produces differences in the opportunities, or life chances, of the social classes.

Examiners' notes

You may need to suggest some reasons for these differences in 17-mark questions. The middle class may marry later and have children later because they tend to stay on longer in education and spend time developing their careers in their 20s. Financial pressures may help explain the higher divorce rate in the working class.

Essential notes

Stronger extended family kinship networks in the working class, if they exist, could be a result of the collectivist outlook of the class, while nuclear families are more individualistic.

Examiners' notes

This issue provides a good opportunity to include evaluation. It is important to stress that inequality lies behind differences between classes, and low income can make it difficult for the working class to achieve a stable family life.

Family diversity and modernity

Introduction

Some sociologists have linked changes in family life to broader social changes in the development of society. One such change is the development of **modernity**. According to some views, early modernity was characterized by fairly stable and predictable patterns of family life in which the **nuclear family** was dominant, but in later modernity greater **diversity** of family types and family relationships were introduced.

Modernity

Some sociologists divide the development of society into three historical time periods:

1. **Pre-modern**, **pre-industrial** society
2. **Modern, industrial society**
3. **Postmodern**, **post-industrial society**.

In pre-industrial societies, life was relatively stable and predictable; people acted on the basis of tradition and roles within society were relatively fixed.

The key change with the development of modernity (modern society) is that social life becomes based upon **rationality** rather than tradition and the teachings of religion. That is, instead of acting in ways that religious leaders tell them to, or in the ways they have been brought up to behave, people calculate how they should act to achieve their goals and this guides their behaviour. The result is that social life becomes less predictable and increasingly uncertain, and more rapid change is introduced.

The **postmodern era** (see page 48) leads to a decline in rationality. More choices are open to individuals and their **identity** become less fixed. This results in even more of the uncertainty and change that was typical of the modern era.

Some of the main changes that have been associated with these eras are summarized in Table 11.

(see page 48)

Essential notes

There is no real debate about the transition taking place between pre-modern/pre-industrial societies and modern industrial societies, but it is disputed whether or not we have entered an era of postmodernity.

Essential notes

The idea that modernity was based upon rationality was introduced by Max Weber (1864–1920) and is the most common way of defining modernity.

Examiners' notes

You will not be required to describe these stages in detail, but you will need to demonstrate an understanding of the basic principles in discussing both theories of the family and of modernity and postmodernity.

	Pre-modern	Modern	Postmodern
Basis of economy	Agriculture	Industry	Services/knowledge economy
Social classes	Landowners/serfs	Bourgeoisie/proletariat	Classes lose significance
Main belief system	Religion/tradition	Science/rationality	No dominant belief system
Main source of identity	Family	Social class	Diverse and image/lifestyle based. Ethnicity and sexuality become more important
Geographical basis of social life	Local	National	Global

	Pre-modern	Modern	Postmodern
Family life	Traditional with marriage as the cornerstone	Marriage and nuclear family central but increasing instability develops	Greater choice and variety develops in sexuality and families and households

Table 11
Stages in the development of Western societies

Other sociologists do not believe that we have yet entered a postmodern era but that we still live in modern societies. Their views are examined in this section. According to these sociologists, families have changed as a result of the changes taking place in the modern era (modernity).

Giddens – relationships in the modern world

Anthony Giddens (1992) believes that intimate relationships have changed with modernity.

- In the early period of modernity in the 18th century, the idea of romantic love developed and marriage became more than an economic arrangement. The marriage partner was idealized as someone who made perfect a person's life.
- In more recent phases of modernity (Giddens calls this **late modernity**), **plastic sexuality** has developed. This means that sex can be for pleasure, and relationships and marriages are no longer seen as necessarily permanent.
- Marriage is now based on **confluent love** – love is dependent upon partners benefiting from the relationship. Couples no longer stay together out of a sense of duty if they are not fulfilled in the relationship, so **divorce** and relationship breakdown become more common.

People in late modernity are involved in a **reflexive project of self** – they constantly think about ways of improving their own life. Tradition and societal **norms** no longer tie couples together as they once did.

Beck and Beck-Gernsheim – individualization

Ulrich Beck and Elisabeth Beck-Gernsheim (1995) see **individualization** as the main characteristic of modern life. This involves:

- More opportunities for individuals, especially women, to take decisions about their lives.
- Little security or intimacy in the everyday world of work, so people seek emotional security in families.
- No generally accepted formula or recipe about love, relationships or family life, so people have to work out their own solutions.
- Conflict resulting from the increased choice and uncertainty and also from the pressures of work life.
- Increased uncertainty, which leads to chaotic personal relationships and helps to explain high **divorce rates**.

Examiners' notes

The ideas of Giddens are useful in answering questions asking you to explain increasing diversity, and questions about changing relationships within the family. Because they add theoretical depth, they can help you get into the highest mark band for both 17- and 33-mark questions.

Essential notes

Beck sees these changes as part of the development of a 'risk society' in which people increasingly face risk and uncertainty from man-made problems rather than from hazards in the natural world. Like Giddens, Beck helps to explain both increasing diversity and changing relationships.

Postmodernity, diversity and the family

Postmodernity and a diverse society

Theories of **modernity** such as those of Anthony Giddens and Ulrich Beck (page 47) imply some move towards **diversity**, but theories of **postmodernity** place an even greater emphasis on increasing diversity, including family diversity.

The main features of postmodern society are as follows:

- A rejection of any grand theory which tells people how to live their lives. The postmodernist Jean-François Lyotard (1984) calls this 'incredulity towards **metanarratives**' – by which he means a lack of faith in any big stories about how society should be run or people should live. This includes a lack of belief in political ideologies such as Marxism, and even a lack of belief in traditional views on marriage and family life.
- Increasing diversity, choice and fragmentation in social life. People have the ability to choose from a vast array of **identities** and lifestyles and do not have to conform to the way previous generations lived.
- Divisions based on **social class** or traditional **gender roles** become much less important while lifestyle choices become much more important.
- The media and the images presented in the media become more influential in a **media-saturated society**.
- Society changes rapidly as new technology is introduced and improved communications lead to a globalization of social life.

Stacey – the postmodern family

The American sociologist Judith Stacey (1996) believes that the postmodern family has developed in the USA. She describes the postmodern family as, 'contested, ambivalent and undecided'. Stacey believes that in the **modern** era families were judged on the heterosexual **nuclear family** as the norm and the closer a family was to that norm the more it was valued. In the postmodern era she sees families as 'diverse, fluid and unresolved'. In other words they:

- are very varied in the structure and form they take
- are constantly changing
- have no set structure that is regarded as the ideal.

For example, gay and lesbian families (part of increasing **sexual diversity**) have to work out their own set of relationships since they cannot model themselves entirely on the heterosexual nuclear family. This means family relationships have to be negotiated between the members. Stacey believes that this makes these relationships slightly more nurturing for children than heterosexual relationships.

According to Stacey, in the USA more than 6 million children were being brought up in gay and lesbian families, making them a significant addition to the variety of family types in that country. Stacey believes there is increasing diversity within gay and lesbian relationships. She points out

Essential notes

Marxists are hostile to postmodernism because they believe that class is still very important in society.

Examiners' notes

You can use this material if you are asked to discuss sexual diversity. It provides a theoretical explanation so it gives you plenty of scope for analysis marks.

that some same-sex couples are asserting their rights to have a fairly conventional family life, raising children in stable relationships based upon legally recognized same-sex marriages, while others have much less conventional lifestyles.

Key study

Stacey's ideas are based upon her study of families in Silicon Valley in California, an area that specializes in the production of computer technology and silicon chips. She sees this as a typical **post-industrial** and postmodern region.

Stacey uses the following example of two families/kinship networks to illustrate the nature of postmodern families.

Pam and Dotty both married manual workers at the end of the 1950s. Both their husbands worked their way up until they had middle-class levels of income, and the women did some unskilled manual work to boost family income. Both were unhappy with the lack of contribution their husbands made to family life, and Dotty was physically abused by her husband. In the 1970s, Pam and Dotty started courses at a local college where they met and were exposed to feminist ideas.

Pam got divorced and started a degree, later getting remarried to a man with whom she had a more equal relationship. She also befriended her first husband's live-in lover to form an unusual **extended kinship network**.

Dotty split up with her husband as well but after he had had a serious heart attack and was no longer physically able to abuse her she took him back. Dotty started campaigning for the rights of battered women and her husband was now expected to do most of the housework. When her husband and two of her adult children died, Dotty formed a new household consisting of herself, one of her surviving daughters – who was a single mother – and four grandchildren.

According to Stacey, Pam and Dotty's families demonstrate the fluid and constantly changing family and household structures in Silicon Valley, which are typical of postmodernity.

Examiners' notes

This case study lacks the large sample necessary to be able to make generalizations. Silicon Valley may not be typical of other areas in the USA, never mind the UK. Making such points can help you get more evaluation marks, especially in 33-mark questions.

Evaluation of postmodern theories of the family

Stacey's study can be criticized for:

- research based on a very small sample of families
- exaggerating the degree of fluidity and uncertainty in family life by picking untypical examples
- underestimating the continuing appeal of heterosexual nuclear families.

However, postmodernism does provide explanations for the increasing diversity of family types discussed in earlier sections of the book.

The New Right and family diversity

Introduction

Postmodernists such as Stacey (see previous page) welcome increasing **diversity**. However, from some viewpoints increasing diversity is undesirable because traditional **nuclear families** are the most stable type of family and are useful to society. This viewpoint is adopted by the New Right, who believe that increasing diversity reflects declining moral values.

New Right views are associated with the ideas and policies of political parties. In the UK, New Right thinking influenced the policies of the Conservative governments of Margaret Thatcher and John Major between 1979 and 1997.

The New Right's perspective strongly supports **free-market capitalism**. It believes that the state should intervene as little as possible in the economy, leaving **private enterprise** to generate wealth. From this viewpoint competition benefits consumers and society as a whole by driving down the price of goods, while driving up the quality. New Right thinkers see markets as based on choice and believe they encourage individual liberty.

The New Right and the family

However, New Right theorists do not see choice and liberty as being so important in terms of family life. Instead, they see traditional nuclear families as the cornerstone of stability in society. They favour traditional families for the following reasons:

- They see them as encouraging self-reliance – family members help each other rather than relying on the state.
- This helps to reduce state expenditure on welfare (for example, for lone parents).
- They see families as encouraging shared moral values and believe they are the best way to pass down morality to children.

Unlike functionalists, they do not believe that the family is a stable institution, performing universal functions for individuals and society as a whole. Instead they see it as increasingly unstable, leading to increases in social problems.

The New Right and policies

When Margaret Thatcher was in power some policies were introduced to try to support traditional nuclear families. For example, in 1988 taxation was changed so that cohabiting couples could no longer claim greater allowances than married couples.

Pamela Abbott and Claire Wallace (1992), however, argue that some of Thatcher's policies allowed or even encouraged people to live outside the traditional nuclear family. For example, divorce laws made it relatively easy for married couples to break up, welfare payments made it possible for mothers to be single parents, and 'illegitimate' children were given the same rights as those born to married couples.

Examiners' notes

New Right perspectives have similarities to the functionalist view of the family but put more emphasis on free-market economics. They can be useful for evaluating perspectives on the role of the family in society.

Examiners' notes

This highly conservative view of families, which sought to prevent changes in family life, contrasted with the radical policies of Margaret Thatcher's governments which changed many other aspects of society and the economy.

Abbott and Wallace believe that Margaret Thatcher's government only introduced a limited range of policies to support nuclear families – the main emphasis was on saving money.

The decline of the nuclear family?

Some New Right thinkers such as Patricia Morgan (2003) believe that there is strong evidence of a decline in the traditional nuclear family as diversity increases.

Key study

Patricia Morgan collected a range of statistics apparently showing that nuclear families were under threat. These included:

- An increase in **cohabitation** amongst couples whether they have children or not.
- An increase in the proportion of children born outside marriage. (Government figures show a rise from 37% in 1997 to 45% in 2008.)
- An increase in the divorce rate.
- Evidence that suggested cohabitation was more unstable than marriage, as cohabiting couples were more likely to split up than married ones.
- The decline in the **fertility rate**.
- An increase in the proportion of the population living in a one-person household.

Criticisms of New Right perspectives

- Advocates of family diversity such as Robert and Rhona Rapoport (1989) see increasing diversity as a good thing because it gives people greater freedom to live in the household or family type that best suits them.
- Some sociologists believe that New Right thinkers exaggerate the extent to which family life has changed.
- **Feminists** believe that the increase in divorce and lone parenthood can be beneficial for women escaping violent, abusive or exploitative relationships with men.
- Postmodernists see the declining dominance of nuclear families as part of wider changes in society that are unlikely to be halted by changes in government policies and are in some ways desirable.

Conclusion

New Right perspectives are characterized by fear of changes in the family that result in a decline in nuclear families. New Right thinkers believe that the traditional nuclear family is the key to a stable and well-ordered society and yearn for a return to those traditional family structures. However, it seems unlikely that the trend towards diversity, which is actually welcomed by many sociologists, will be reversed in the near future.

Essential notes

Although most of the statistics used by Morgan are accepted, the interpretation of them is not. The changes she describes can be seen as evidence of increasing diversity in families, rather than a decline in stability or in the acceptance of family values. The New Right interpretation can be used to contrast with the views that support increasing diversity.

Examiners' notes

The critique of this perspective can be developed further by providing more details of the alternative views of other perspectives, such as feminism and Marxism, which are highly critical of the New Right.

Social policy and family diversity

Introduction

The family has sometimes been regarded as a private sphere in which the state should not interfere. However, there is no doubt that in the UK a number of state policies have both a direct and indirect impact upon family, and that the government sometimes deliberately tries to intervene in aspects of family life. For example, the state can affect family life through:

- education policies such as the provision of nursery education and compulsory schooling
- taxation policies such as the way the incomes of husbands and wives are taxed
- legal changes such as changes in divorce law or child protection legislation
- housing policy such as the size and location of social housing
- health and welfare policies such as 'care in the community', which affects the responsibility of families for relatives.

Sometimes these policies are based upon the assumption that people should live in traditional **nuclear families**, sometimes that **diverse** family types should be supported, and sometimes they are more ambiguous.

Sociological and political perspectives on the family
The New Right

As discussed earlier, the **New Right** are strongly in favour of conventional nuclear families where married heterosexual couples live with their children. They support nuclear families because they see them as providing stability and regard them as independent and self-reliant. If family members care for each other (for example, families taking care of elderly relatives), this reduces state expenditure and allows taxes to be kept low, which benefits private enterprise. They also believe that nuclear families pass on a work ethic to their children and this benefits free-market economies.

Charles Murray (1984) argues that an **underclass** has been created through over-generous welfare payments, especially to lone parents. Single parenthood is an aspect of diversity which New Right thinkers regard as harmful to society because it encourages irresponsible behaviour amongst children who copy their parents. Sons of single mothers lack an adult male role-model of a hard-working and responsible father taking care of his family. Daughters of single mothers may follow in the mother's footsteps by having children out of wedlock, often while they are young, and then relying upon state benefits to support them.

The causes of the underclass

- Benefits allow unmarried lone-parent mothers to raise children
- Young unmarried women become single parents
- Fathers don't take responsibility for children
- Lack of adult role models
- Unemployed young fathers unwilling to work
- Young men on benefits turn to crime.

Essential notes

It is worth bringing in feminist views to evaluate perspectives that are critical of diversity. Feminists are highly critical of New Right views because they are based on the assumption that male breadwinners are necessary for successful socialization. Feminists believe that diversity gives more choice to woman and stops them being trapped in patriarchal families.

The New Right influenced the policies of Conservative governments between 1979 and 1997, particularly in the period when Margaret Thatcher was in power.

Feminist views

As discussed on page 28, feminists are critical of the nuclear family, arguing that it is usually **patriarchal** and biased in favour of men. Feminists believe that social policies generally act to maintain the power of men in families and do little to control men who are violent or abusive to their partner or children. Feminists therefore tend to favour policies that give more choice to women, including liberal divorce laws and tax and benefits policies that make women independent of their male partners. They are therefore more sympathetic to family diversity.

Key study

An example of feminist research on social policy and family is provided by Eileen Drew (1995), who argues that the policies of different governments follow different **gender regimes** (sets of policy which make different assumptions about family life). There are two main types of gender regime:

- **Familistic gender regimes** favour and support traditional nuclear families in which husbands are expected to be the main breadwinner while wives are expected to concentrate on domestic responsibilities.
- **Individualistic gender regimes** have more egalitarian policies, believing that assumptions should not be made about the roles of husbands and wives and that they should be treated equally. This type of gender regime is more tolerant of the choices that individuals make and is more accepting of diversity in family life.

Drew argues that many countries are moving towards a more individualistic gender regime. Whether this is the case in the UK will be examined below.

Examiners' notes

To add theoretical substance to the content of answers to both 17- and 33-mark questions, it is useful to refer to different types of gender regime.

Policies supporting conventional families

A number of policies which support conventional families (or familistic gender regimes) have been identified by sociologists. These include:

- The assumption that child benefit should usually be paid to mothers.
- The organization of schooling – the early finishing time assumes one parent will be at home in the afternoon, making it difficult for **dual-earner families**.
- Limited state provision of care for the elderly and the encouragement of relatives (usually daughters) to care for elderly relatives.
- According to Fox Harding (1996), housing policies tend to assume that nuclear families should get priority over lone-parent families, who are then given less desirable social housing.

☞ This topic continues on the next two pages

- Child support policies have emphasized the importance of absent parents (usually fathers) paying for their offspring. The Child Support Agency was set up in 2003 to pursue maintenance payments and was replaced in 2008 by the Child Maintenance and Support Commission.

Policies more supportive of diversity

Some state policies in the UK have not supported conventional nuclear families. Instead they appear to favour **individualistic gender regimes** and therefore diversity. These include:

- The gradual liberalization of **divorce** laws (see page 21).
- The recognition of gay and lesbian relationships.
- Increased provision of state funding for childcare for children under school age. (The New Labour government provided two and a half hours of childcare per weekday for all three- and four-year-olds.)
- Increasing police action and concern about domestic violence, particularly that committed by men against women.

Policies and political parties

The extent to which recent British governments have followed an approach to families that generally favours conventional, single-earner nuclear families has been examined by sociologists.

New Right governments, 1979 to 1997

According to Pamela Abbott and Claire Wallace (1992), the governments of Margaret Thatcher and John Major did follow some policies supporting traditional families. For example, they:

- changed taxation policies so that **cohabiting** couples could no longer claim more in tax allowances than married couples.

However, they also:

- did not introduce tax or benefits policies to encourage mothers to stay at home
- made **divorce** easier to obtain in 1984
- gave illegitimate children the same rights as those born within marriage.

Abbott and Wallace conclude that in reality they had a more balanced approach to families than their ideology would suggest.

New Labour, 1997 to 2010

The New Labour party, which was in power from 1997 to 2010, followed the New Right in arguing that the traditional family was a desirable institution, particularly for bringing up children. However:

- New Labour was more willing to accept that family diversity was the norm and that policies should reflect this.
- They allowed **civil partnerships** for gay and lesbian couples and also allowed these couples the right to apply to adopt children.

Essential notes

Whatever the philosophy underlying the policies of different parties, in the end most tend to limit their interventions in family life.

Essential notes

John Major's government introduced a 'Back to Basics' campaign extolling the virtues of conventional morality and family life, but it was undermined when the infidelity of some cabinet ministers was exposed.

This suggests that New Labour adopted a more **individualistic gender regime** than the Conservative government.

However, New Labour did introduce a number of policies to strengthen conventional families. For example:

- They gave employees the right to time off work for family reasons.
- They introduced a Working Families Tax Credit to help families with their finances.

Jennifer Somerville (2000) points out that even though Tony Blair's government recognized diversity, it idealized family life as a 'working example of mutual interdependence, care and responsibility' and increased expectations about parental responsibility.

Coalition government from 2010

In 2010, David Cameron became Prime Minister in a coalition government between Conservatives and Liberal Democrats. Cameron promised before the election to introduce tax breaks for married couples, suggesting something of a return to support for conventional nuclear families. However, at the party conference in 2010, it was announced that Child Benefit would be stopped for families with a higher-rate taxpayer. This disadvantages affluent families with a single earner and a stay-at-home parent – **dual-earner families** can earn much more than single-earner families without losing the benefit.

Conclusion

All political parties have extolled the virtues of nuclear families, but once in power all recent governments have had to acknowledge the reality of increasing family diversity. None have succeeded in reversing a move away from traditional gender roles in conventional nuclear families and towards greater diversity in family and household types.

Essential notes

Ann Oakley was a pioneering feminist sociologist who was the first to study housework systematically. She clearly showed the limitations of the work of Young and Willmott, who could be accused of putting forward **malestream** (mainstream, **patriarchal**) views. This research is dated now, but more recent research provides some evidence that inequalities still exist.

Examiners' notes

Examiners will always be impressed with methodological evaluations of research. When using this or other survey research, it is worthwhile mentioning that the reliability of the research is always questionable. For example, it has been demonstrated that men and women often given different answers when asked about who does household tasks, so it is difficult to know how reliable any set of figures is.

Conjugal roles, housework and childcare

Types of conjugal role

Conjugal roles are the roles of husband and wife within marriage.

Two main types of conjugal role have been distinguished:

1. **Segregated conjugal roles**. The roles of husband and wife are very different. The husband is the main **breadwinner** and has little involvement with housework and childcare. Husbands tend to spend leisure time away from the family with male friends, while women spend more time with female kin such as their mothers and sisters.
2. **Joint conjugal roles** involve men and women doing some paid work and also both spouses being involved with housework and childcare. Typically, with this type of conjugal role, men and women spend more time together and less time with their own groups of same-sex friends.

These two types of conjugal role are extremes and often roles will be somewhere in between.

The symmetrical family

Michael Young and Peter Willmott (1973) claim that joint conjugal roles were becoming more common in the **symmetrical family**. They found a move towards greater equality within marriage in that wives were now going out to work and husbands were providing more help with housework.

These views were heavily criticized by Ann Oakley (1974), who noted that in Young and Willmott's research, a family was regarded as symmetrical if the husbands did any housework at least once a week. This hardly represented equality within a household. Her own research found that few men had high levels of participation in housework and childcare, with only 15% of men contributing significantly to the housework and 30% to the childcare.

Survey research on conjugal roles

Larger-scale research using survey methods provides more reliable data on the **division of labour** within the home. The British Social Attitudes Survey has collected data over a number of years and found some shift away from traditional roles in the 1980s and early 1990s. However, in more recent years there has been little change. In 1994 women always or usually did the laundry in 81% of households; by 2006 this fallen just 4% to 77%.

% saying task 'usually or always' done by women	1994	2002	2006
Laundry	81	81	77
Shopping for groceries	42	46	42

Table 12
Gender and domestic tasks – 1994–2006 in Britain

Childcare

Mary Boulton (1983) argues that who does which task does not adequately represent the burden of responsibility within households. She argues that even when men help more with childcare, it is still mothers who take the main responsibility for their children and who have to prioritize their children above other aspects of their lives. The National Child Development

Survey (1996) found it was still very unusual for fathers to take prime responsibility for childcare.

Time

Another way to study **gender roles** is to examine time spent on different tasks. This gives an indication as to whether men or women spend more time on paid and unpaid work.

Jonathan Gershuny (1999) examined data from 1974–5 and 1997 to look at long-term trends. He found there had been a gradual shift towards men doing a higher proportion of housework, but in 1997 women continued to do more than 60% of the domestic work even when both partners were working.

The British Time Use Survey (2005) found that women spent a total of 3 hours 32 minutes per day on housework and childcare, whereas men spent on average 1 hour 56 minutes on these tasks. Men did, however, spend more time on paid employment. Nevertheless, on average, men had 1 hour 32 minutes per day more leisure time than women. The difference was less great for **cohabiting** men and women (because men living without a partner tend to have more leisure time than women without a partner since they are less likely to be responsible for children).

	Male	Female
Cooking, washing up	27	54
Cleaning, tidying	13	47
Washing clothes	4	18
Repairs and gardening	23	11
Caring for own children	15	32
Paid work	211	132
Watching TV & video	170	145

Conclusion

The evidence suggests there continue to be significant differences in the conjugal roles of husband and wife, although the degree of inequality may be reducing over time. Men continue to do fewer household tasks, take less responsibility for childcare and have more leisure time than women.

Examiners' notes

Boulton's study can be used as an example of how the validity of research in this area can be questioned. Statistical data might not truly reflect the nature and extent of the burden of childcare for each parent.

Examiners' notes

Remember to point out some of the strengths of research as well as the weaknesses. Surveys such as this can be seen as relatively reliable because of their large sample size and the careful way in which samples are collected.

Table 13
Time in minutes spent on main activities by sex, 2005

Essential notes

Conjugal roles will vary considerably between individual couples and social groups. For example, research generally shows that **working-class** marriages tend to be less equal than **middle-class** marriages, and there will certainly be differences between **ethnic groups** in their conjugal roles.

Conjugal roles, power and emotion work

Power and decision-making

The most common way to measure **power** in households is through an examination of decision-making.

A study by Irene Hardill et al. (1997) examined power in dual-earner households in Nottingham using interviews. Households were classified into those where the husband's career took precedence in making major decisions, those where the wife's career took precedence and those when neither career was deemed more important than the other. In 19 households the man's career came first, in five the woman's career came first and in six neither was prioritized. Thus men continued to be dominant in the majority of households.

Power and money

Power can also be measured in terms of control over money in the household. Jan Pahl (1989) studied 102 couples with children and classified households into four types, as shown in Table 14.

Examiners' notes

In common with a number of other studies in this section, you can gain extra marks by commenting on the unrepresentative nature of the sample. In this case, it is not known that dual-earner households in Nottingham will be typical of the rest of the country.

Examiners' notes

Economic power is seen as particularly important both by Marxists and by Marxist-feminists. It is useful to make these theoretical links in answering questions on conjugal roles and also useful to use evidence such as this in answering theory questions on Marxism and feminism.

Pattern of management	Number of households	Type of decision-making	Degree of inequality
Husband-controlled pooling	39	Money was shared but the husband has the dominant role in choosing how it was spent	Gives men greater power
Wife-controlled pooling	27	Money was shared but the wife has the dominant role in choosing how it was spent	Gives women greater power
Husband control	22	Husband usually has the only or main wage and gives his wife housekeeping money or allowance	Usually leads to male dominance
Wife control	14	Wife has overall control of the finances, perhaps giving her husband an allowance. Most typical in low-income households which relied upon benefits	Appears to give women more power, but in many cases they are struggling to pay the bills on low income, making financial management a burden

Table 14
Control over money in households – Jan Pahl

Pahl found that wife-controlled pooling led to the most equal relationships, but this pattern is most often found in low-income households.

Only just over a quarter of the couples have a system that was fairly equal, suggesting men continue to be dominant.

Research by Heather Laurie and Jonathan Gershuny (2000), using data from the British Household Panel Survey (1991 and 1995), showed movement away from the housekeeping allowance system which tends to make males dominant. Over this period, the proportion saying that male and female partners had an equal say rose from 65% to 70%. Equality was more likely where women had high earnings, but overall men still have more economic power.

Conjugal roles and emotion work

Jean Duncombe and Dennis Marsden (1995) believe that any measurement of inequality within households must take account of **emotion work**. Emotion work involves thinking about the happiness and emotional well-being of others and acting in ways that will be of emotional benefit to others. It might include:

- complimenting other people
- smoothing over arguments
- buying presents and cards for birthdays
- planning activities which others will enjoy
- smiling at a baby.

Duncombe and Marsden believe that women perform a **triple shift**, not only doing most of the housework and childcare, and doing their fair share of paid work, but also doing the vast majority of the emotion work. Their study involving interviews with 40 couples found that many women were dissatisfied with their partner's emotional input. Many believed that their emotion work helped to keep the family together.

Lesbian households

Gillian Dunne (1999) studied roles within lesbian households, in many of which there was a dependent child. Unlike heterosexual households, responsibility for childcare was fairly equally shared rather than being largely the responsibility of one partner. Household tasks were also fairly equally shared in more than 80% of the cases studied.

Dunne concludes that masculine and feminine roles in society tend to lead to hierarchical relationships and male dominance. Without these **gender roles** greater equality is much easier to achieve.

Conclusion

Most of the evidence suggests that women are still far from achieving equality within marriage in Britain today.

- They still do the majority of the housework.
- They still take the main responsibility for childcare.
- They still have less time for leisure than their male partners.

However, there is some evidence of change over time and, in terms of the total amount of hours per day spent on work of one kind or another, differences between males and females are no longer that great.

Examiners' notes

This is a large-scale study so the data is quite reliable. It hints at the variety of relationships within households, so remember to point out that there are a wide range of different arrangements affected by factors such as class and how much paid work each partner does.

Examiners' notes

This study, and the concepts of the triple shift and emotion work, have been widely quoted and it is important to learn these concepts for the exam. The concept of emotion work adds an extra dimension to our understanding of family life, although some people may feel that it is stretching the definition of 'work'.

Examiners' notes

This section can be used to support the **feminist** view of the family, particularly the radical feminist view, which sees violence as a way of maintaining **patriarchy**. It can also be used to criticize the **functionalist** view which does not acknowledge the 'dark side' of family life.

Domestic violence and abuse

Types and definition

The main types of violence and abuse in families are:

- Violence and abuse perpetrated by one adult partner against another (usually called domestic violence).
- Violence and abuse perpetrated by adults against children (child abuse).

The Home Office (2000) defines domestic violence as 'any violence between current or former partners in an intimate relationship wherever and whenever it occurs. The violence may include physical, sexual, emotional, or financial abuse.'

This broad definition is generally given for **domestic abuse**. A narrower definition of **domestic violence** includes physical and sexual violence but not emotional or financial abuse.

The extent of domestic violence and abuse

Fig. 10 shows that reported domestic violence rose considerably between 1981 and 1996, although it has gradually declined since then.

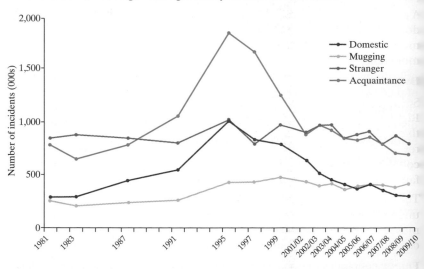

Fig 10
Reported domestic and other abuse in England and Wales, 1981–2010

The British Crime Survey produces figures on domestic violence and other forms of abuse. The 2009/10 survey found that in the previous 12 months in England and Wales:

- four women in every thousand were a victim of domestic violence
- two men in every thousand were a victim of domestic violence.

This survey also found that 7% of women aged 16 to 59 were victims of domestic abuse (physical, emotional, psychological or financial abuse) compared with 4% of men.

Research by James Nazroo (1999) suggests that domestic violence perpetrated by men against women tends to be more serious than that perpetrated by women on men, and women are likely to be much more fearful of the violence than men are.

Examiners' notes

It is useful to comment that these figures may underestimate the true extent of domestic violence and abuse since many victims may be unwilling to admit that it has taken place.

The British Crime Survey is based on a large sample of over 40 000 people so it is quite reliable, but it only covers England and Wales and people aged 16 or over so the scope of the statistics is somewhat limited. The validity of the data may be open to question since it can be a matter of interpretation whether abuse has taken place.

Explanations of domestic violence and abuse

Feminism

Radical feminists such as Erin Pizzey (1974) see domestic violence as resulting from **patriarchy**. In a male-dominated or patriarchal society, men use violence or the threat of violence in order to control women. Pizzey also argues that domestic violence is widely tolerated and often not seen as a serious crime. Patriarchal values lead to female partners being seen as essentially the property of their male partners, and therefore using violence to control them is seen as partially acceptable.

Fiona Brookman (2008) believes that the nature of **masculinity** is partly to blame. In our culture masculinity values control over others so men can resort to violence if they feel they are losing control over their female partner. Her research was based on in-depth interviews with violent men.

A problem with this approach is that it does not explain the existence of domestic violence perpetrated by women against men. Social attitudes may also have changed, with domestic violence seen as less acceptable and more likely to result in prosecution.

Dysfunctional families

Some conservative commentators associated with the views of the **New Right** believe that domestic violence takes place in **dysfunctional families**, that is, families which do not function well. Their view is that violence results from the instability of families caused by factors such as increasing **cohabitation** and **divorce**, and the decline in moral standards in some families, particularly those from lower social classes.

This view suggests that feminists exaggerate male violence and underestimate female violence. It is criticized by feminists who believe that male violence against women is both much more serious and much more common than female violence against men.

Emotional intensity and family life

Anthony Giddens (2006) argues that it is the nature of family life that makes domestic violence quite common. Family life is characterized by 'emotional intensity and personal intimacy', meaning that it is normally charged with strong emotions, often 'mixing love and hate'. In these circumstances, even minor arguments can escalate into acts of violence. The increasing isolation of the **nuclear family** from **extended kinship networks** may be increasing this intensity.

A problem with this argument is that it does not explain why violence is common in some families but not others.

Conclusion

Relationships between parents and children in families vary considerably from family to family and are influenced by factors such as **class**, ethnicity, sexuality, and family and household type.

Examiners' notes

It is useful to comment here that **liberal feminists** recognize that there may have been some improvements in the treatment of victims of domestic abuse and violence. Referring to different feminist perspectives can help to get you in the top mark band.

Examiners' notes

To critique this view you can suggest that there is little evidence to support it and it may be based largely on the political views of the writers.

Examiners' notes

You could choose any two of these reasons to answer 17-mark questions. Giddens' views could be evaluated with reference to studies on the changing nature of extended kinship networks. Since they appear to remain important (see page 8), you can use the research to criticize Giddens.

Examiners' notes

The New Right, particularly writers such as Charles Murray, believes that lone parents are poor parents because they set a bad example to their children (see page 42). However, their ideas have been heavily criticized. Incorporating theory and evaluation such as this can get you in the top mark band, particularly for 33-mark questions.

Parents and children

Child-centeredness

Hugh Cunningham (1976) believes that three principles form the basis of contemporary parenting:

1. Children should be separated from the adult world.
2. Children can be corrupted through exposure to adult life and they need to be protected from it.
3. The happiness of children is paramount.

Essential notes

Jenks' views are very similar to those of Anthony Giddens (see page 47) and it is worth mentioning this. Both Jenks and Giddens offer rather generalized views without much research to back them up. Both of them neglect the variations in relationships within families, for example, between different ethnic groups.

Key study

Jenks: Postmodern childhood

Chris Jenks (2005) believes principles such as those outlined by Cunningham have led to **child-centred** parenting. This type of parenting results in the needs of children within families taking priority over the needs of adults. The nurturing of children is seen as more important than the well-being of adults.

Jenks relates this to the development of **postmodern** childhood. In postmodern societies identities have been destabilized so that people no longer have a secure, grounded sense of who they are. Family life is insecure with frequent **divorce**. In these circumstances, children have become the final source of **primary relationships** – the most fulfilling and unconditional relationships. Wives and husbands and partners have become disposable, but children are not and the parent–child bond is therefore the most important in society. Children become subject to increased surveillance because parents are more fearful for their children and determined to protect them.

Examiners' notes

Postman's ideas have some similarity with the views of the **New Right** that traditional family life is under threat because morality has been undermined in a more liberal society. You could criticize Postman by arguing that he exaggerates the degree to which children were sheltered from adult life and sexuality in previous eras because he provides little evidence to support the view that they were sheltered in this way.

Key study

Postman: the disappearance of childhood

Neil Postman (1994) takes a very different view of changing relationships between parents and children. He claims that the distinction between childhood and adulthood has been eroded in recent years so that childhood no longer exists as a distinct stage in the **life course**. He believes the disappearance of childhood is due to the growth of the mass media, which has exposed children to the adult world of sex, violence and suffering via television and the internet. Parents can no longer protect children from exposure to the adult world, so that children grow up quicker and their behaviour becomes less regulated by their parents at an earlier age than in the past. This reduces the distinctiveness of parent and child roles within the family.

Jenks: the continuing distinctiveness of childhood

Jenks does not believe that childhood is disappearing as a distinct stage in the life course. Jenks points out that children continue to be highly regulated and restricted by laws which control behaviour in public spaces, the consumption of alcohol and cigarettes, education, sexuality, political rights and so on. Laws prevent children from taking up adult roles until they reach specific ages, and parents play a large part in enforcing these rules.

Changing gender roles and fathers

Other sociologists have identified more specific features of changing parent–child relationships.

Examiners' notes

This evaluation is particularly useful in 33-mark questions on changing parent–child relationships in the family.

- Chapman (2004) believes that parent–child relationships have changed considerably as a result of the increase in the proportion of married women in paid employment. In the 1960s, working mothers were criticized for 'neglecting' their children, but now it is seen as better for children to go to nursery and mothers to do paid work. This change has also led to fathers becoming more involved in childcare.
- Research by Esther Dermott (2003) into 25 fathers with professional or managerial jobs found a new style of 'intimate fathering' where men sought a closer, more emotional and more open relationship with their children.

Examiners' notes

This research can be criticized with reference to feminist theory that men do little **emotion work**.

The increasing involvement of fathers in parenting does not necessarily mean that mothers and fathers play the same role in parenting.

- A study by Backett (1987) found that mothers still took the lead in deciding the main features of childcare, and mothers still interpreted the needs of children for their husbands. Fathers found it difficult to interpret their children's needs and to act on them themselves.
- Research by Carol Smart (1999) into 60 couples who got divorced found only one in which parenting was fully shared between mothers and fathers before divorce. Even after divorce, many mothers continued to advise their former spouses about how they should relate to their children.

Good and bad parenting

There is some evidence which suggests that the standard of parenting has improved over recent decades with parents becoming more able to meet the needs of their children.

Examiners' notes

Don't forget to gain analysis and evaluation marks by evaluating research. In this case, the sample size is large, suggesting the research is reliable, but there is no way of checking how accurate the diaries are.

- A study by Jonathan Gershuny (2000) involving 3000 parents keeping diaries of their activities found that the amount of time parents spent reading to or playing with their children had quadrupled over recent decades.
- On the other hand, Sue Palmer (2007) claims that parents increasingly use television and electronic games to keep children entertained and they put less effort and time into interacting with their children.

Parents may still be abusive or cruel to their children or neglect them. In 2009, 16 900 children in Britain were placed on child protection orders for neglect, and 50 children were found to have died as a direct result of parental neglect or abuse.

The ageing population

The ageing population can impact on family roles and responsibilities.

Changes in the age structure

The **age structure** refers to the proportion of people in different age groups in a population. **Population pyramids** (such as Fig 11) illustrate the relative proportions of different age groups for these segments.

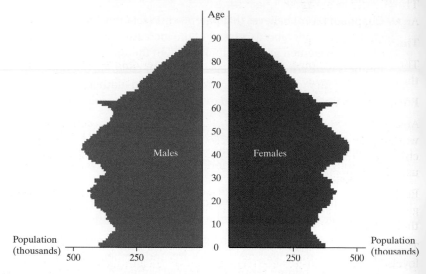

Fig 11
Population by gender and age, UK, mid-2009

Traditionally, population pyramids tend to be triangular, narrowing in older age groups, but recent trends in the UK have produced an ageing population.

Fig 12 shows that between 1984 and 2009, the percentage of the population over 65 increased from 15% to 16%, while the percentage of under 16s decreased from 21% to 19%.

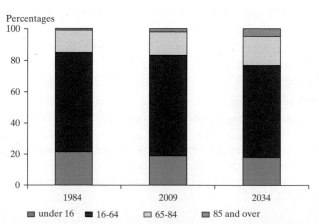

Fig 12
Population by age, UK, 1984, 2009 and 2034 (projection)

On projected trends, by 2034, 23% of the population will be over 65, while just 18% will be under 16.

The **median** age increased from 35 years in 1984 to 39 in 2009, and is projected to rise to 42 by 2034.

Reasons for the ageing population

- The falling **death rate** – people tend to survive more years after adulthood, leading to a growing number of elderly.
- The falling **birth rate** and **fertility rate** – means fewer children.

The effects of an ageing population

An ageing population can have a number of effects.

The dependency ratio

The rising proportion of the population beyond retirement age increases the economic burden on those of working age.

Effects on families

An ageing population can place extra economic burdens on adults of working age, who may need to care for elderly parents as well as raising children. This burden tends to fall particularly heavily on women, who usually end up being the main carers.

Research by Emily Grundy and John Henretta (2006) found that a 'sandwich generation' of women often end up caring for their own elderly parents and their grandchildren simultaneously.

There is a strong cultural assumption that as families age, the primary loyalty of adults transfers from their parents to their own children. Dorothy Jerrome (1993) discusses how elderly parents can become frustrated by lack of access to and time with their children.

However, the effects are not all negative:

- Grandparents can provide valuable support by helping to care for grandchildren. This can help to strengthen **extended kinship networks**.
- As Jerrome says, grandparents are likely to be fit and active and play a full part in the life of the family.
- Julia Brannen (2003) believes **intergenerational** links between grandparents and their chidren and grandchildren are strong in the increasingly important **beanpole family** (see pages 9 and 37).

Government spending

Provision for the welfare of the elderly imposes a large burden upon the government owing to their demands on healthcare. In response, the government has restricted the amount of support for care of the elderly and has started to raise retirement ages.

Social problems for older people

An ageing population will result in households consisting of single pensioners. The number of retired people living in **poverty** is likely to increase.

However, the health of older people has been improving: more remain economically active and place less burden on health and social services.

Examiners' notes

It is important to emphasize in answers that an ageing population can be the result of low birth and fertility rates just as much as it can be a result of increasing life expectancy.

Essential notes

There is material on page 12 covering the reasons for the falling fertility rate and smaller family size.

Essential notes

It is useful to make a link to feminism here: a number of feminists have studied the ways in which the care of elderly parents restricts the life chances of women.

Examiners' notes

The examiner will be impressed if you get some balance into your answer by showing that there are some positive aspects to the ageing population.

General tips for the Sociology of the Family exam

The 'Topics in socialization, culture and identity' examination paper is made up of two 2-part questions on each topic: Family, Religion, Health and Youth. You will have one and a half hours, and are required to answer two 2-part questions on one or more topics. The first of each 2-part question, part (a), is a 17-mark question which tests your knowledge and understanding of the topic. This question always starts with the instruction to 'Identify and explain two reasons (or factors/ ways/trends, etc.)'. You should spend approximately 15 minutes on this question and aim to write approximately three-quarters to one side of A4. To achieve the top band marks for part (a) questions, two points need to be identified and then explained using relevant sociological evidence including theories, concepts, studies and contemporary evidence. You are advised to think carefully about which two points to select so that you demonstrate a range of knowledge and understanding. You need to identify two clear and distinct factors with explanations that do not overlap. Using a separate paragraph for each point identified and explained is a useful way to be clear that you have offered two different points.

Common errors on part (a) questions which result in many students not achieving the top mark band are:

- Failing to explain the two points fully; often simply identifying and giving only a brief explanation.
- Failing to make use of sociological theories, concepts and/or contemporary evidence to develop the answer and demonstrate sociological knowledge and understanding.

You must also be careful to avoid producing unnecessary introductions before answering the question, identifying more than two points, identifying two points that overlap to such a degree that they can only be treated as one point, and including explanations that have little relevance to the point identified.

The second part of each question, part (b), is an essay-style question, worth 33 marks. This question always starts with the instruction 'Outline and evaluate' and is often followed by a specific view or theory. You should aim to spend approximately 30 minutes on this question and aim to write about two sides of A4. As this is an essay question, you are tested on all three assessment objectives:

1 knowledge and understanding
2 interpretation and application
3 analysis and evaluation.

There are 11 marks available for each of these assessment objectives.

To achieve the highest marks in the skill of knowledge and understanding, you need to include sociological evidence, i.e., theories, concepts and/ or accurate contemporary evidence on various sides of the argument. It is important that you show a detailed understanding and that you are able to write in an informed way.

To achieve the highest marks in the skills of interpretation and application, you should select and apply different types of data, including theories, concepts and/or contemporary evidence on various sides of the argument. You should identify the most relevant data and then show how this relates to the question, highlighting patterns and trends, supported with evidence where appropriate. Using phrases like 'This study shows ...', which explicitly use the wording of the question, can encourage application to the question.

In terms of analysis and evaluation, you should write in a way that shows that you have engaged with the different views involved in the question and that you understand the various elements that make up each of the views. A sustained evaluative approach can be demonstrated by writing an evaluative introduction, making some relevant evaluative points about studies, theories and ideas, and summarizing the different views in relation to the question. You should aim to evaluate specific sociological arguments from more than one side of the view, based on the available evidence, methods and explanations. It is helpful if you use key terms to signal that you are assessing the evidence or the argument at that point; for example, 'however', 'on the other hand', 'conversely', 'on the contrary', 'in contrast'.

Some common errors to watch out for on answering part (b) questions are:

- Insufficient sociological knowledge, relying on anecdote or drawing from common sense. (Better responses make use of sociological theories, concepts and/or studies.)
- Answers that are well informed sociologically but use material that is of only marginal relevance to the question on the paper.
- Relevant data selected but not applied to the question, leaving a list-like response that does not answer the question sufficiently.
- Failure to interpret and apply sociological data; for example, statistics and findings of sociological studies or examples from current events or broader social trends.
- One-sided answers that only consider evidence agreeing or disagreeing with the view.
- Juxtaposed arguments or evidence with little explicit evaluation. (Better answers offer critical comments, weighed up arguments and evidence and draw a reasoned conclusion about the view.)
- Part (b) answers that are only a little longer or even shorter than their part (a) answers. (Don't forget that part (b) requires a response that is at least twice as long as part (a), reflecting the marks allocated.)

To summarize, you must ensure that you know how long to spend on each part of the exam and time yourself accordingly. You also need to be aware of the assessment objectives targeted in each part (b) question and select relevant, sociological points which can be explained in some detail.

Sociology of the Family (sample exam questions 1)

1 (a) Identify and explain **two** reasons for the growth in single person households in the contemporary UK. [**17 marks**]

   (b) Outline and evaluate the view that the traditional nuclear family is the best family type. [**33 marks**]

[**Total: 50 Marks**]

2 (a) Identify and explain **two** ways in which an ageing population affects family life. [**17 marks**]

   (b) Outline and evaluate the view that the family is characterized by diversity in the contemporary UK. [**33 marks**]

[**Total: 50 Marks**]

On pages 70-73 you will find student answers to these questions which result in an overall grade C. Examiners' comments explore what the answers do well and not so well, and how this candidate could have improved their responses.

Sociology of the Family (sample exam questions 2)

1 (a) Identify and explain **two** changes in patterns of marriage in the UK. [**17 marks**]

   (b) Outline and evaluate the functionalist theory of the role of the family in society. [**33 marks**]

   [**Total: 50 Marks**]

2 (a) Identify and explain **two** reasons for the increase in cohabitation in the contemporary UK. [**17 marks**]

   (b) Outline and evaluate the view that relationships between men and women in the family are becoming more equal. [**33 marks**]

   [**Total: 50 Marks**]

On pages 74-78 you will find students answers to these questions which result in an overall grade A, together with examiners' comments.

On pages 80-81 you will find more help to show how to improve your answers to the shorter (part a) questions for the Sociology of the Family exam.

An accurate point has been identified. It is more than basic as there is use of sociological evidence in the form of concepts and a study/theory, but it lacks the depth needed for the highest band. For example, the point could have been linked to postmodern society.

Another accurate point has been identified with some explanation. This response uses references to contemporary examples as a form of sociological evidence but could have been developed with support from different types of evidence; for example, statistical evidence on women in the workforce or women's pay. The candidate could have brought in feminism as a theory to support the point about women's independence. Concepts such as feminization of the labour market and Sharpe's study on women's changing priorities would also support the point about women having skills and opportunities and so don't need to be married.

Overall, there is good knowledge and understanding, but not enough developed explanation to get into the top band.
Mark 11/17

Grade C answer

1 (a) *Identify and explain **two** reasons for the growth in single person households in contemporary UK.* [17 marks]

In 2005, 29% of all households consisted of a single person. This is three times the amount of forty years ago. One reason for such an extensive increase is the growth of individualism in modern day society. This is Gibson's idea that people are selfish now and are more interested in their own needs, concerns and freedoms than the compromise that comes with living with a partner and/or children. Because of this, many people prefer living alone, even if they do pursue relationships at the same time.

An additional potential reason is the emancipation of women. Nowadays women don't need to be married in order to have financial support, as they have the skills and are given the opportunities to do it themselves. Furthermore, due to changes in the law, women can now own their own property whereas previously, only males could. At least partly because of this, many women have decided that living independently is the best thing for them and thus it has become quite common.

(b) *Outline and evaluate the view that the traditional nuclear family is the best family type.* **[33 marks]**

The traditional nuclear family consists of two heterosexual adults and two to three offspring. They should all live together and the adults' relationship should be based on a romantic love. Some functionalists would say that this is the best family type and is the dominant ideology; however, others such as Goode argue that it is just the ideal type, but that other structures also work.

They believe that it serves several important purposes. Some of which are described in Parsons' 'warm bath' theory. He says that the first purpose is 'primary socialization' of children; this means that children are taught the value consensus in the family, i.e. the norms and values of society. The second purpose Parsons focuses on is the 'stabilization of the adult personality', which is the suggestion that the family provides the emotional support and a place to relax, away from the pressures or working life that adults need. He says that without the family, adults would become overwhelmed and unstable, thus threatening society. The family also is an agent of social control. It controls members' behaviours so that people don't start rebelling and committing socially unacceptable acts whenever they want – it teaches them what's right and what's wrong. Another important part of the family is its economic functions. The two incomes of the parents are used to provide for the children and because they are living together, the living cost is cheaper per person than it would be individually.

Other perspectives would criticize this overly optimistic view of the family. Feminists say that the nuclear family emphasizes gender difference and is ruled by men, with them being the dominant figurehead. Marxists disagree with basically all of functionalists' ideas about the family. Instead of it being a good thing that the family socializes their children into society, Marxists see it as another generation being brainwashed into believing in the oppressive capitalist system. Furthermore, in rebuttal to Parsons' theory of stabilization of the adult personality, they say that the family is a place for workers to take out their frustration. This often leads to domestic abuse. They think that the family is destructive and should be abolished as the only people that really benefit from it are the ruling classes who get to continue exploiting workers.

Postmodernists on the other hand say families are so diverse now that the traditional nuclear family doesn't really exist and generalizations cannot be made.

A good introduction which defines the key concept in the question (nuclear family), although this could have been developed by, for example, including reference to the nature of the conjugal roles. Some good analysis and evaluation is shown by recognizing different views on the value of the nuclear family.

The candidate explains Parsons in depth, using sociological concepts and clear explanations and examples. However, the functionalist view is underdeveloped and evidence narrow in range. The response could be improved by adding more focus to nuclear families, rather than just the family in general. The role of the traditional nuclear family in gender role socialization is an important feature as it includes heterosexual parents who take on gendered roles as instrumental and expressive leaders of the family. There is also a lack of range of knowledge and understanding of views that support the view; for example, New Right theories and other functionalist views.

This is explicit evaluation of the view in the question and displays knowledge of the counter arguments, although it could include supporting studies or concepts. Counter-arguments need supporting evidence; for example, Marxist-feminist Ansley's view on women's role in the family. This would add range and depth.

In terms of interpretation and application it is not focused enough on the nuclear family specifically; it is discussing the family in general. The last point about postmodernism is a relevant one and could have been developed further. ☞

Overall, there is good knowledge and understanding but it does not reach Level 4 as there is a lack of range of other theories or evidence supporting the view in the question and a lack of depth on the counter arguments, which are presented in a list-like way.
Mark 6+8+7 = 21/33

Overall mark for parts (a) and (b) = 32/50

---

2   (a) *Identify and explain **two** ways in which an ageing population affects family life.* [**17 marks**]

The level of older people in Britain has increased significantly in the last thirty years – 29% from 1971 to 2004. An ageing population could affect family life in both positive and negative ways. Largely, which way depends on their level of independence.

Ginn and Arber have suggested that class, ethnicity and gender all affect how useful an older person can be to their family and society. For example, a middle-class individual is more likely to be fit and active than a lower-class person due to diet and lifestyle. Therefore the healthy middle-class person could continue to help out their family through things such as childcare whereas someone from the working class could potentially just become a financial burden. So, for some families the availability of childcare is a positive aspect of the ageing population. It would mean that children do not have to be paid for to go to day care and can spend more time in a family environment.

But on the other hand, due to modern medicine, sick older people can be kept alive for longer. Whilst families generally do whatever they can to keep their elderly relatives alive, this can become very expensive to both the state and individuals. Having to pay out thousands of pounds to keep someone alive usually falls to their children, which can have detrimental effects on said child's own family, not only financially but also emotionally.

The candidate has correctly identified social differences in relation to how an ageing population affects family life and focuses on childcare provision. To develop this point, it would have been useful to have some further sociological evidence to support this; for example a study or some statistics.

This point focuses on the financial burden of an ageing population, but it lacks depth and is a little anecdotal (e.g. 'costs thousands of pounds'). This needs much more precise sociological evidence to back it up.
Overall, two ways have been identified with some sociological concepts and evidence, but it is narrow and underdeveloped.
Mark: 9/17

---

2   (b) *Outline and evaluate the view that the family is characterized by diversity in the contemporary UK.* [**33 Marks**]

Most sociologists accept that there has been a massive increase in family diversity in the last 100 years. Postmodernists celebrate the rise in family diversity while other theorists, including some Functionalist and New Right thinkers, argue that the extent of diversity is exaggerated and that the nuclear family is still the most sought after family type.
The Rapoports have identified several different areas of how family diversity can be characterized in modern Britain. The first of which is 'organizational diversity'. This is the way in which families have different structures; for example, step-families, single parent families, beanpole families etc. ☞

This is a good introduction which sets out the debate in theoretical terms. There is a clear for/against argument selected and it demonstrates the skill of interpretation and application by applying theories to the specific question.

The second type of diversity is 'cultural diversity', which is how different families in society have different cultures and values. Part of this is Berthoud's continuum which says that generally Pakistanis and Bangladeshis have old-fashioned values and so they have high rates of marriages and low divorce rates; Caribbeans show the most modern individualism with least marriages, most divorces and highest rates of single mothers. Whites are also fairly 'modern' but not as much as Caribbeans, and Indians/Asians are fairly 'old fashioned'. Another type of diversity is 'class diversity'. The Rapoports say that there may be a difference in the way families behave towards each other between the classes. For example, parents tend to be more child-centred in the middle classes. This is backed up by evidence from Frank Furedi. They also say that working-class children are less likely to have a satisfactory upbringing due to poverty, greater crime rates in their areas and so on. The fourth type of diversity is said to be 'regional diversity' – there are disproportionate patterns of family life in different areas of Britain; for example, more retired people near the south coast. This was shown in a study by Eversley and Bonnerjea. There is also 'life cycle diversity'. This is the way families change as they get older, in terms of childcare, income and number of people in the family. The final type is 'sexual diversity'. Research suggests that same-sex relationships are very different from heterosexual ones; for example, they have higher levels of equality as they do not have gender stereotyped jobs to do.

While the Rapoports give these different types of structures, feminists believe that the family is not so diverse as they all seem to have a common theme of patriarchal systems which solely benefit men. Marxists also believe there is some but not so much diversity, as everyone still works to the capitalist system of oppression to the lower classes. Allen and Crowe on the other hand agree with the Rapoports and say that there is a continuing growth of diversity in the family, so much so that there is no longer a clear family cycle and in fact everyone is individual.

In conclusion, from the evidence above it is clear that there has been a definite shift in the levels of diversity in Britain but it is not fair to say that every family is unique and there are some cultures in which there doesn't seem to be much more diversity than 100 years ago.

This shows good knowledge and understanding of a classic study on family diversity, displaying depth of understanding of different types of family diversity. Notice how the response links to other studies in a relevant way, again demonstrating both knowledge and understanding and the skills of interpretation and application. There are some missed opportunities to develop the answer in greater depth; for example, Furedi's view could be explained.

This is explicit evaluation of the view in the question and the candidate attempts a theoretical interpretation. However, the evaluation lacks depth of explanation and the interpretation of the theories is underdeveloped. There is no mention of the New Right or Postmodernists, which was signposted in the introduction.

This is an explicit attempt at a conclusion, but it is a little vague; what does it mean by 'some cultures'? In the UK or elsewhere? Note that the question is specifically about the contemporary UK so global issues of family diversity are not really relevant.

Overall, this response is more than basic as it includes sociological evidence in the form of studies and theories but it lacks in range and depth of knowledge and understanding, and it is a little one-sided. Evaluation is explicit but a little superficial.
Marks: 6+7+7 = 20/33

Overall mark for parts (a) and (b) – 29/50
Overall mark – 61/100 Grade C

Grade A answer

1 **(a)** *Identify and explain **two** changes in patterns of marriage in the UK.* [17 marks]

This paragraph explains one identified change – people delaying getting married. Notice how the candidate clearly identifies the point and then explains it. The explanation includes a range of sociological evidence in the form of concepts, contemporary examples and a study.

One change in the pattern of marriage is that people are choosing to marry at a later age. This can be explained by changes in social policy in recent years. For instance, the Equal Pay Act and the Sexual Discrimination Act allowed women to achieve a lot more economic freedom and independence in the workplace, and they are therefore less likely to need to marry at an early age due to the pursuit and potential rewards of a career. Women in particular, therefore, choose due to the improvements in pay and better treatment by male authorities, to prioritize their careers over starting a family or committing to someone through marriage. This is backed up by the studies by Sue Sharpe. She interviewed girls in the 1970s and then again in the 1990s. She found that their priorities had changed from 'love, marriage, family' to 'job, career and being able to support themselves'. Also, economic benefits to getting married have also decreased due to the introduction of the Welfare State, and the removal of tax benefits for married couples in the 1980s, so a couple may choose simply not to marry to save themselves potential economic marginalization.

Again, the second point is clearly identified and well explained, using sociological concepts, studies and examples from the media.

Overall, this response is a Level 4 answer which shows a very good knowledge and understanding of two changes in patterns of marriage. It is slightly unbalanced with more explanation being provided for the first point.
Mark: 15/17

The second pattern is that the marriage rate is declining. Developments in social expectations and standards may contribute to the amount of people choosing not to get married, as the standards with which people consider a marriage are too high for an ordinary relationship to withstand. Fletcher argues that the current decline in people getting married is in fact not correlative to its decline in importance, but its increase in value. The influence in the Hollywood film ideology of romanticizing a marriage into an unrealistic relationship has caused many relationships to not make it to the altar as they cannot live up to the expectations promoted by the media. Another ideological movement that could influence decisions to get married is the feminist movement, as women accept their alternative choices to marriage a lot easier than before. Alternatively, people may decide not to marry for practical reasons; it is so expensive.

1 **(b)** *Outline and evaluate the functionalist theory of the role of the family in society.* [33 marks]

This is a very detailed introduction that clearly outlines the theoretical debate which targets interpretation and application marks. Note also how the candidate offers an explanation of some of the general principles of functionalism before applying it to the family, which demonstrates some depth of understanding of sociological theory.

Functionalism as a theory stresses that all aspects of society must work together in order for society to function best, each area being vital to the essential workings. In order to keep all these different functions working, a value consensus that is important to all members of society helps to influence their behaviour by the means of social control. Essentially, according to functionalists, the family is a key component in enforcing this value consensus and emphasizing the importance of other institutions in society. Increasingly, functionalist views have been criticized by feminists and Marxists, who see their views as out of date and supporting the patriarchal family.

Parsons, a key functionalist, states that the nuclear family has become the key to socializing both adults and children into valuable and hard-working ☞

members of the whole community. In pre-industrial society the extended family was really important with whole families working and living closely together. The family was responsible for a whole range of functions such as looking after the elderly, educating children and providing health care. When industrialization occurred, other parts of society developed to take over some of these functions, such as the NHS and the education system. Parsons calls this process structural differentiation. The nuclear family developed as a result of these changes and its small structure is ideally suited to modern societies. In this sense, Parsons argues that the nuclear family 'fits' the needs of a modern industrial society.

Nowadays the main role of the family is essentially primary socialization, the teaching of the value consensus being crucial for the next generation's personalities and motivations, ensuring that they are feeling a part of the community and subsequently working hard for the benefit of society. Secondly, the family serves to 'stabilize the adult personality'. This means it provides a sense of security and stability to men who come home from a hard day at work to find their wives and children ready to provide practical and emotional support. Parents can relieve their tensions by playing with their children and engaging in joint activities such as watching TV.

Another functionalist writer is Murdock. He argued that all societies contain nuclear families because they provide certain crucial functions for all societies. They work together or economically co-operate in some way; for example, the husband has paid work while the wife cares for the home and children. Like Parsons, Murdock also argues that the nuclear family is essential in socialising children. He also states that nuclear families are necessary to organize and control sexual activities and the reproduction of the next generation.

Functionalists have come in for a great deal of criticism, particularly from perspectives that are more critical of the nuclear family. Feminists believe that functionalism is an outdated ideology that justifies the traditional gender stereotypes of a caring mother at home and dominating father in paid work – functionalists ignore the way nuclear families oppress women and are often violent and abusive. They point to all the hidden cases of domestic violence that go unreported, for example. Marxists such as Ansley are also critical of the way nuclear families control their members and provide a way of reproducing the labour force for capitalists. Postmodernists too attack functionalists by saying that they ignore family diversity. Nuclear families are declining and functionalism does not seem able to accept that other types of family might work too.

In conclusion, functionalism has helped understand the development of the nuclear family but is now out of date in that it focuses almost exclusively on the nuclear family and doesn't recognize that family diversity is a feature of contemporary British society.

This is a detailed explanation of Parsons' theory, which uses contemporary examples as an illustration of the theory. It is conceptually strong and focused well on functionalist theory. However, there are missed opportunities for evaluation; for example the 'fit theory' has not been questioned, or Parsons' view that the family performs two main functions.

It is useful to be able to discuss another functionalist in addition to Parsons, and Murdock is clearly related to the functionalist theory. The candidate does well to focus on the role of the family in society rather than discussing it more generally. Again, there is no direct evaluation of Murdock's work.

This paragraph is evaluative in tone, criticizing the functionalist perspective from other theoretical viewpoints. It is sophisticated in that alternative theories are directly related to functionalism and are not just given as juxtaposition. However, it would have been good to bring in a wider range of evidence; for example, more studies to support the counter arguments.

This is an attempt at an explicit conclusion and it does offer a further criticism of functionalism as outdated. However, it could have been developed further in terms of highlighting the main strengths and weaknesses. ☞

Overall, this essay demonstrates a very good knowledge and understanding of functionalist views of the family and counter-arguments are presented clearly. Appropriate evidence is selected and applied to the specific question, but this is slightly less developed in the evaluation. This is a relevant and coherent essay which addresses both sides of the debate, although evaluation is not sustained throughout the essay.
Mark – 8+11+7 = 26/33

Overall mark for parts (a) and (b) – 41/50

The first reason is clearly identified and then explained with depth and detail. Notice how the answer is kept well-focused on cohabitation. There are accurate sociological concepts included (stigma, secularization) and contemporary examples as well as research-based evidence (2001 census). This is a good response.

2 (a) *Identify and explain **two** reasons for the increase in cohabitation in the contemporary UK* **[17 marks]**

One reason for the increase in cohabitation is secularization. This means that religion is no longer as significant to society and individuals as it once was. In terms of cohabitation, it is now not considered as 'living in sin' if you live with your partner outside of marriage, and people are not as likely to believe that you will 'burn in hell' should you choose to have sex or children with your partner outside of wedlock, in a relationship of cohabitation. This means that there is no longer a negative stigma attached to cohabitation. According to the 2001 census, young people with no religion were more likely to cohabit than those with a religion. Therefore if, over time, people are becoming less religious, they will not be influenced by religious-based morality on issues including cohabitation and marriage. This is all part of what sociologists refer to as changing social attitudes. There is a decline in stigma attached to cohabitation and this is reflected in the decline of religious belief.

Once again, the second point is clearly identified and explained. The candidate has introduced some theory and made it relevant to cohabitation and it is conceptually very strong. There is also a reference to a study (Gibson), which makes it more wide ranging in terms of knowledge and understanding.
Mark: 17/17

A second reason for the increase in cohabitation is the postmodern idea of individualism. Now, people's decisions regarding living situations and relationships are defined by individuals' freedom of choice. Gibson states that the concept of personal satisfaction and gain in all aspects of people's lives, including relationships, is influencing feelings of obligation to decrease. So, in order to maintain an individual stance, people have cohabited increasingly, as they are able to have a relationship whilst still being more able to better themselves as individuals. Commitment is more of a fluid concept, as relationships have become more changeable, with people moving from relationship to relationship in order to get what they want as an individual out of a relationship. The living together method of cohabitation is much more compatible with this new concept, as there are no legal or familial disputes, and it allows the individual to carry on benefitting themselves as much as they see fit. Therefore, cohabitation's association with individualism has probably contributed to its increase.

2 (b) *Outline and evaluate the view that relationships between men and women in the family are becoming more equal.* **[33 marks]**

The term conjugal relationships describes the relationship between husband and wife within the family. It is suggested by some March of Progress sociologists, such as Willmott and Young, that relationships between men and women in the family are becoming more equal or symmetrical. In such families, there is more negotiation and sharing out of tasks such as roles in childcare, domestic and emotional roles in the household. Functionalists, such as Parsons, on the other hand, argue that conjugal roles were not equal as men should take on an instrumental role and women should take on an expressive role. A Marxist's perspective would dispute this idea, and argue that the roles were unfairly split in societies' quest of exploitation of the family in order to prevent revolution and maintain the ruling class's power. Feminists highlight in particular the exploitation of women in the face of equality between men and women in the family, and the effects of their increasing workload.

In terms of equality in childcare, the role of fatherhood in the family has arguably become increasingly more important to a male identity, as is argued by many sociologists. Burghes states that the responsibility of emotion work with children has become more important to men than their role as the breadwinner of the family. However, what must be considered is whether this in effect puts more pressure on the women to maintain the economic income. Thompson's study of working fathers found that 80% were happy to stay home from work and look after their infant children. However, there has been no evidence of these men compromising their breadwinner role for their role as a father in practice. But, Dermott also states the role of 'intimate fathering' is much more of a social expectation of men, contributing to Gershuny's theory that the family is becoming more symmetrical in women's acceptance of paid work and men consequently participating in more domestic activities. This theory originated from Young and Willmott's idea of the symmetrical family, developing from the breakdown of the extended family and the focus on the nuclear family and its functions being split equally between men and women. The financial decision-making aspect of conjugal roles is reportedly subject to class not gender, as Pahl found that in working class families, women typically control the finances. A Marxist view of these findings would conclude that this is due to the exploitation of the working class males that the females have to compensate for their lack of capacity to deal with financial issues.

Inequality within relationships between men and women is, however, a frequently argued issue still by sociologists. Dunscombe and Marsden dispute the positivity in women's increasing participation in paid work as they state that their other responsibilities still remain. So, women end up enduring a triple shift of domestic work, paid work and emotion work within childcare. It is argued that this inequality is so significant that they end up working much larger amounts of hours than men do. This is actually highlighted by Elston's study of male and female doctors, in which he found that the responsibility of childcare and domestic work still fell under female control despite both genders having the same demanding career. DeVault is perhaps a bit more compromising ☞

A detailed introduction; maybe a little too long as it loses the central debate; that is, whether relationships are becoming more equal between men and women. However, it is good to offer a theoretical overview as this targets both interpretation and application marks as well as evaluation and analysis.

This is a good paragraph; notice how evidence is explained and then questioned or criticized which gives the sense of sustained evaluation. This paragraph is full of relevant studies and evidence.

However, this section could be developed in a little more depth. It reads as if rushed and is a little unclear in places.

Similarly to the last paragraph, there is a very good level of knowledge and understanding given in the form of studies and concepts, with some theory included. Notice how there is some evaluative tone throughout this paragraph with the candidate considering other viewpoints. However, like the last paragraph, it is a little rushed in places at expense of depth.

with her ideas about equality, as she states that women are in fact not responsible for all the work, but have an additional amount of work that is not appreciated as work itself, invisible work. This would typically include shopping and cooking, taking up a considerable amount of time but not seen as hard work. Opposing the functionalist idea of the family taking the role of 'stabilization of the adult personality', feminist Ansley claims that 'women are the takers of shit', enduring larger amounts of work than men, not benefitting at all from the functions of the family. The alleged increase in the importance of the fatherhood role is disputed by Gatrell with the idea that men in fact assert themselves in their childcare role to defend their dominance over the family as a whole. Also, in terms of decision-making, Edgell recognizes the differences between the decisions men make, the important financial decisions, and those women make which are in fact more frequent on a daily basis but are considered less consequential and in turn less significant.

When considering the equality between men and women in the family, the arguments suggest that despite increases in opportunities for women to participate in more male-orientated activities such as paid work, the expectations of women are still higher. So, perhaps it is more fitting to consider the individual expectations of genders themselves. Dunne found that in homosexual relationships there is much more negotiation of roles and work, and in turn equality. Therefore, it is likely that it is not the family as an institution that has a problem with equality, but heterosexual relationships themselves, as they seem to contain more male domination.

This is a good conclusion which is reflective and analytical in tone. It is a good idea to really bring the question back into focus in the conclusion, and here the candidate questions the family as a site for equality.

Overall, this is a well-structured essay with both range and depth of knowledge and understanding; very slightly underdeveloped in parts. Very well focused on the question, displaying a very good ability to interpret appropriate sociological knowledge and applies it effectively. Analysis and evaluation is wide-ranging and sustained. However, it didn't achieve top marks as it is somewhat unclear and lacks clarity in places. It feels a little rushed and it is underdeveloped in parts.
Mark: 9+ 11+ 9 = 29/33

Overall mark for parts (a) and (b) – 46/50

Overall mark = 87/100 Grade A

Improving your grade

The following examples show how you can improve your answers to the shorter part (a) questions in the Sociology of the Family exam.

A basic response which is lacking in depth and range of knowledge. Time is wasted at the beginning of the answer by stating the trends, whereas the question asks for the reasons for these trends. Two reasons are identified but there is very little explanation of each reason. There is a tendency towards anecdote ('old people don't want to live alone') unsupported by sociological evidence (in terms of concepts, studies or theories) and sociological ideas are marginally related.
Mark 6/17

Part (a) question

1   *Identify and explain **two** reasons for the growth in single-person households in the contemporary UK.* **[17 marks]**

Weak answer

There has been a big rise in the number of people living alone and the figure has increased 3 times. One reason for the growth in single person households is that women outlive men and therefore there are more female pensioners living alone. These old people don't necessarily want to be alone; their spouse has died at an earlier age. This can then cause a burden on society.

Another reason for the growth in single person households is that women are now more independent than ever before and they are choosing to live alone as a sign of their independence. This is linked to women getting married later and having children later too.

Two reasons are identified, with more detailed explanation than the answer above. There is some evidence offered, in the form of statistics and concepts, although it would be better if the evidence were sourced to a sociological study. For example, who says that it is more socially acceptable? Also, the second reason is actually a combination of two different reasons – changing position of women and changing social attitudes. The candidate does attempt to link these, but it is advisable to stick with one identified point and develop it. This is a Level 3 response, although it is relatively narrow and underdeveloped.
Mark 10/17

Better answer

One reason for the growth in single-person households is because of the increase in separation and divorce. This creates more single-person households, particularly among men under 65. In fact, the largest growth of single-person households has been within younger populations, particularly in the proportion of men between the ages of 25 and 44. This is because, following divorce, any children are more likely to live with their mother, and the father is more likely to leave the family home and live on his own, with some access to his children. This is, however, likely to be a temporary phase as statistics show that many men in these situations go on to form new relationships and families and therefore stop living alone.

Another reason for the growth in single-person households is the increased choice available to people, especially women. In the past, a woman would be labelled a 'spinster' if she lived alone, but it is now much more socially acceptable. Today, many people see living alone as a positive lifestyle option where the family is becoming less central to people's lives.

Good answer

One reason for the growth of single-person households is because of changing social attitudes. Historically, people living alone were either viewed with sympathy or, particularly for women, were stigmatized as 'spinsters'. Today attitudes are changing and many people see living alone as a positive lifestyle option. According to Hall, many people who live alone do so by choice. They value the freedom and independence which living in a one-person household provides. Most have active social lives and many are involved in close relationships; they just don't live together. Duncan and Phillips refer to this as LATs (Living Apart Together) and it is an increasing trend in contemporary society. This trend reflects postmodernists' belief that individuals are much more free to pick and choose their identities and their living arrangements. Peter Stein calls it 'creative singlehood', which is the deliberate choice to live alone.

Another reason for the growth of single-person households is related to geographical mobility. Younger one-person households are concentrated in large cities, such as Manchester, Liverpool, Sheffield and particularly London. Many are young professionals who migrate to cities to find employment as the growth in professional, managerial and technical jobs are concentrated in the large urban areas. According to Hall, of the young professional migrants to London, 62% of men and 53% of women live alone. One-person households are expensive. Two people together can live more cheaply than two people separately. However, professional and managerial jobs are well paid and, as a result, people in these jobs can afford to live alone.

Two reasons are identified and well explained. There is a range of sociological evidence, including concepts (for example, LATs, creative singlehood, geographical mobility), theories (postmodernism) and studies (for example, Hall). However, it is imbalanced in the sense that the second reason lacks depth, compared with the first.
Marks: 15/17

Sociology of the Family

Achieved status	A position in society which affects the way others view you that is earned at least partly through your own efforts, e.g. a job
Ageing population	A situation in which an increasing proportion of the population in a given country is middle-aged or older
Alienation	A sense of being distanced from something so that it feels alien, e.g. feeling a lack of connection and fulfilment in work
Ascribed status	A position in society which affects the way others view you that is given by birth, e.g. being male or female
Beanpole family	A family in which links between generations, i.e. between grandparents, parents and grandchildren, are strong but links with other relations such as aunts, uncles and cousins are weak
Birth parent	The woman who gives birth to a child, whether or not the child was conceived using her egg
Birth rate	The number of live births per thousand of the population per year
Bourgeoisie	The **ruling class** in **capitalism** who own property such as capital, businesses and shares
Breadwinner	The person doing all or most of the paid work in order to pay for the expenses of a family
Capitalist society/ capitalism	A society in which people are employed for wages and businesses are set up with the aim of making a profit
Cereal packet image of the family	The image of the family often presented in marketing as a conventional heterosexual **nuclear family** of legally married couples with one or more (but not too many) children, with a male **breadwinner** and a female housewife
Child-centred	A situation in which the interests of children are put before the interests of adults
Chosen families	Groups of people who are treated like and seen as family members even when they are not related by blood or marriage; friends can be members of chosen families
Civil partnership	A legal partnership of two people, whether homosexual or heterosexual, with similar rights and responsibilities to a marriage
Class/social class	Groups within society distinguished by their economic position and who are therefore unequal, e.g. the middle class in better paid non-manual jobs, and the working class in less well-paid physical jobs
Class diversity	The variations in family life that result from differences in **class subculture**
Class subculture	The distinctive lifestyle associated with a particular **class**
Cohabitation/ cohabiting	Lliving together in an intimate relationship without being married
Cohort	A group of people born within a particular time period
Competition	When individuals or businesses try to do better than one another, e.g. in selling more goods than another company
Conflict theory	Theory of society which sees one or more groups in competition for scarce or valued goods. Examples include Marxism and **feminism**

Confluent love	Love which is dependent upon partners benefiting from the relationship rather than on unconditional devotion
Conjugal bond	The relationship between husband and wife
Conjugal roles	The roles of husband and wife within marriage (it may also be applied to male and female partners who cohabit but are not married)
Consensus theory	Theory of society which assumes that the same interests are shared across society, meaning that there is little conflict
Cultural diversity	Differences in family life that stem from differences in lifestyle and beliefs, e.g. from religion
Death rate	The number of people dying per thousand of the population per year
Dependency ratio	The number of people in non-economically active age groups (children and the retired) relative to the size of the population of working age
Difference feminism	Feminism which emphasizes that the position of women in society varies and women cannot be seen as a single, united group
Division of labour	The way in which jobs are divided up between two or more people, e.g. who does particular tasks in a household
Dispersed extended family	Kin who keep in touch with one another but are geographically spread out
Diversity	Variety in social life
Divorce	The legal ending of a marriage
Divorce rate	The number of people who divorce per thousand married people in a population per year
Domestic abuse	Actions which are damaging to current or former partners in an intimate relationship; this can include physical, sexual, emotional or financial abuse
Domestic labour	Work done within the home such as housework and childcare. It may be unpaid but it creates value just as paid work does
Domestic violence	Actions involving the use of force or the threat of force against current or former partners in an intimate relationship which are harmful to the other partner. Domestic violence need not take place within the home but can take place anywhere
Dual-earner families	Families in which both partners are in paid employment
Dysfunctional families	Families which do not function well for family members or in fulfilling social roles, e.g. they fail to socialize children adequately
Economic base	In Marxist theory, the foundation of society consisting of the economic system
Economic function	The role the family plays in providing food, shelter and the ability to consume products for its members
Economic unit	A household which shares its resources amongst the household members and is relatively independent from other households
Educational function	The role of the family in providing a stable environment in which children can be socialized into the culture of their society
Emotion work	The time and effort involved thinking about and acting to produce the emotional well-being and happiness of others

Empty-shell marriage	A marriage where the partners continue to live together but the emotional attachment and sexual relationship have come to an end
Ethnic group	A group within a population regarded by themselves or by others as culturally distinctive; they usually see themselves as having a common origin
Extended family	The family wider than the nuclear family. As well as parents and children it includes other relatives such as aunts, uncles and grandparents
Extended kinship network	The interrelationships between people related by blood or marriage regardless of whether they live together
Familistic gender regimes	Sets of government policies which support traditional **nuclear families** in which husbands are the main breadwinner and wives do most of the domestic work
Family diversity	The growth of variety in the structure and nature of family types
Female-carer core	According to Sheeran, the most basic family unit consisting of a mother and child/children
Female-headed family	Family with a female head of household, usually without an adult male
Feminism/feminists	Theory of society which claims that women are disadvantaged and exploited by men, while men are dominant and run society in their own interests
Fertility rate	The number of live births per thousand women aged 15 to 44 per year
Fragmentation	Breaking into pieces
Free-market	A system in which businesses can compete with one another without state interference
Friendship networks	Groups of friends who interact with one another without living together
Functionalism	A belief that social institutions serve some positive purpose
Function	A useful job performed by an institution for society
Gay and lesbian households	Households based around male partners or female partners in an intimate, sexual relationship
Gender regimes	Sets of policies which make assumptions about the roles of men and women in family life
Gender roles	The socially expected behaviour of men and women in a particular society
Genetic parent	The parents whose sperm or egg was use to create the child
Geographical mobility	The movements of people to different regions or countries
Heteronorm	The belief that all sexually intimate relationships should be based on heterosexuality
Household	A group of people who share the same accommodation
Housewife	A married or cohabiting woman who has the main responsibility for housework and childcare and who does not do paid employment
Identity	The way people are seen by themselves or others in society
Ideological state apparatus	According to Poulantzas, parts of society which encourage people to accept the values favoured by the **ruling class** and which helped to maintain **capitalist** society
Ideology	A distorted set of beliefs which favours the interests of a particular social group

Izzat	A sense of family honour in some Asian communities
Illegitimacy	Children born to unmarried parents
Individualism/ individualistic	An emphasis upon the desires or interests of individual people rather than those of wider social groups
Individualistic gender regimes	Sets of social policies which do not assume that husbands and wives will follow traditional roles and which accommodate the choices made by individuals regardless of whether they are male or female
Individualization	A process in which the wishes of individuals become seen as more important than the maintenance of traditional norms and values and the prioritization of the interests of individuals above those of social groups
Industrialization	The process whereby manufacturing takes over from agriculture as the most important component in a society's economy
Infant mortality rate	The number of children dying before their first birthday per thousand of live births per year
Isolated nuclear family	A **nuclear family** (parents and children) which is relatively self-sufficient and has few contacts with extended kin
Intergenerational	Between generations, e.g. between parents and children
Intragenerational	Within a generation, e.g. brothers and sisters
Joint conjugal roles	Relationships between husbands and wives in which both do some paid work and both do housework and provide childcare. Typically with this type of role men and women spend a good deal of time together
Kin	People linked by blood or marriage
Late modernity	According to Giddens, the most recent phase in the development of **modernity**
Legitimate	Used as a verb to make something seem fair and reasonable, used as a noun to mean something which is accepted as fair and reasonable
Liberal feminism	A version of **feminism** which is relatively moderate and believes that the position of women in society can be improved through reform rather than radical or revolutionary change
Life course	The development and change in people's lives over periods of time. Unlike **life-cycle** the life course does not have fixed and predictable stages
Life-cycle	The stages of life, e.g. childhood, young adulthood and old age, which are predictable and assumed to be experienced in the same way by different people
Life expectancy	The average age to which a particular group of people is likely to live
Lone-parent family	Family consisting of one parent living with one or more of their children
Macro/theories	Theory which looks at the bigger picture, i.e. society as a whole
Malestream	To **feminists**, something which is mainstream and male-dominated or biased in favour of men
Marital breakdown	The ending of a marriage whether through **divorce**, **separation** or the development of an **empty-shell marriage**
Masculinity	The behaviour and social roles expected of men in a particular culture
Matrifocal family	A family headed by the mother where she is not co-resident with a male partner

Means of production	Those things required to produce goods such as land, machinery, capital, technical knowledge and workers
Median	The middle value in any group, e.g. the median age is the age of the person in a population where half of the people are older than them and half are younger
Micro theory	Theory which examines small-scale aspects of society rather than society as a whole
Media-saturated society	A society in which people's impression of reality is largely shaped by high levels of exposure to the mass media
Metanarrative	A 'big story' about how the world works and how people should live their lives, e.g. a political theory or a religion
Middle class	People who have white-collar jobs which require some qualifications and are generally better paid than **working-class** jobs
Migration	People leaving or entering a country or area to live for a significant time
Modern	Characteristic of or belonging to modernity
Modernity	An era in the development of society characterized by rationality, i.e. planning to achieve goals, and in which the influence of tradition and religion is reduced compared to previous eras
Mode of production	A system of producing things which dominates society, e.g. **capitalism**
Nayar	Members of a society in southern India
Neo-conventional family	A traditional nuclear family, but one in which both the husband and wife do paid work rather than having a single, male **breadwinner**
New reproductive technologies	Technologies which allow previously infertile couples or individuals to have children, e.g. in-vitro fertilization (test-tube babies)
New Right	Politicians, thinkers and writers who support the free-market rather than state intervention and who believe that traditional moral values should be preserved
Norms	Specific, informal rules of behaviour in a particular society
Nuclear family	A co-resident family of two generations: parents and children
One-person household	A person living on their own
Organizational diversity	Variety in the structure of families, e.g. **lone-parent, nuclear** and **extended**
Patriarchy/ patriarchal	Literally 'rule by the father' usually used by **feminists** to refer to a system in which men have more **power** than women and shape how societies run
Plastic sexuality	Behaviour where sex can be for pleasure as well as for conceiving children
Population pyramid	A bar chart representing the distribution of the population in different age groups
Pluralization of lifestyles	A process in which people come to live in more varied ways rather than sharing similar ways of living
Post-industrial	After the phase of society when manufacturing was the dominant part of the economy
Postmodernity/ postmodern	The era following modernity in which rationality becomes less important, image becomes more important and in which many old social divisions break down
Poverty	Lacking the resources to pay for the minimum acceptable lifestyle

Power	The ability of a person to get their own way or to determine outcomes regardless of the wishes of others
Pre-industrial society	Societies that existed before industrialization where most production was based upon agriculture
Primary relationships	The most important and emotionally charged personal relationships, e.g. between parents and children
Primary socialization	The first stage of the process through which children learn the culture of their society. This takes place in the family
Private enterprise	Businesses owned by individuals or shareholders rather than run by the state
Radical feminism	The most extreme version of **feminism** which tends to see society as being completely dominated by men and sees the interests of men and women as being very different
Rationality	Behaviour which is geared towards achieving specified goals rather than based on emotion
Reconstituted family	A family that includes members from previous families which have broken up but which are brought together as two new partners form a relationship
Reflexive project of self	The way individuals constantly think about improving their own lives and developing their identity in contemporary society
Relative poverty	Lacking the resources to pay for a lifestyle which is deemed the minimum acceptable when compared with other people in a particular society at a particular time
Reproductive function	The function of the family in ensuring children are reproduced to enable the survival of society
Ruling class	In Marxist theory, the group who are dominant in society by virtue of their wealth and power
Sandbanham husband	In Nayar society, a visiting husband, usually a warrior. Each woman can have several of these husbands
Secularization	The process whereby religious thinking and religious institutions lose social significance
Separation	A couple living apart without getting divorced. Some separations are legal and formal, but most are not
Sexual diversity	The variations in family types that result from gay, lesbian or bisexual relationships
Sexual function	The function of the family in controlling sexual behaviour through monogamy
Single-person household	A person living on their own
Social mobility	The movement of people between social groups, especially social classes
Socialization	The process through which a person learns the culture of their society
Stabilization of adult personalities	To Parsons, the role of the family in maintaining the psychological health of adults by providing warmth and security and allowing them to act out childish elements in their personality
Status	The amount of esteem in which people are held by others in society
Stepfamily	A family which includes one or more children from a previous relationship

Structural differentiation	The process by which society develops a more complex structure as more institutions develop carrying out major social functions
Structural theory	Theory which examines society as a whole and its major constituent, or structural, parts
Subject class	In Marxist theory the group in society who are dominated by the **ruling class** whom they have to work for because they lack the property to produce goods for themselves. The subject class are exploited by the ruling class
Superstructure	In Marxist theory the non-economic parts of society such as the family which are shaped by the economy and controlled by the **ruling class**
Surrogate motherhood	Where a woman gives birth to a child even though the child is not her genetic offspring (i.e. through in-vitro fertilization)
Surplus value	Profits made by the ruling class
Symmetrical family	A family in which both husband and wife do paid employment and both do some housework and provide childcare
Tali husband	In **Nayar** society, a husband who does not live with his wife or have a significant relationship with her
Triple shift	According to Duncombe and Marsden, the three types of work which create a burden for women: paid work, domestic work and **emotion work**
Underclass	The lowest social class, below the rest of the class structure, often seen as consisting of those reliant upon state benefits
Universal	Found in all societies
Upper class	The highest **social class** in society consisting of those who own wealth or property
Values	General beliefs about what is right or wrong in a particular society
Visiting relationship	A relationship where an adult has a partner but they do not live together
Welfare state	Agencies run or financed by the government to provide for the well-being of members of society, such as education, the health service and social services
Working class	People who do manual jobs which require relatively few qualifications and are usually less well-paid than **middle-class** jobs